THE 5-G SHIFT

EMPOWERING THE CHURCH'S FIVE GENERATIONS
FOR SPIRITUAL REVOLUTION

BART PIERCE

The 5-G Shift
Empowering the Church's Five Generations for Spiritual Revolution
by Bart Pierce

copyright ©2019
ISBN: 978-1-950718-16-0
Printed in the United States of America

cover design by Kiryl Lisenko
The 5-G Shift is available in Amazon Kindle, Barnes & Noble Nook and Apple iBooks.

Contents

Endorsements

Generation 1

Mary Amelia Myers
Age 12

God is Good !!

Tyler Sewell, Age 12
I Love Jesus

Nicolas Calvo-Moraes Age 12
God will always be there for you

Parker 12
James
White
The bible speaks to me, God is unstopable
that's why team Jesus is the best team.

Preston 11 years of age
I felt empty until I
came here

JohnL.8
I am here to
help   people ♥

Kara Brown
age: 1 1

"BE You because
its less harder"

Eliana Haliday age 10
~God loves you!

Lamar age 10
god loveS you

God Spoke to me
that I'll be ok I've been adopted
and why girl I was in foster cm
and going after home after him
Jae'lynn Age 11

5

Generation 2

Celeste Garcia-Rivera
Age: 14

"When you experience the presence of God, just recieve his words and plans for you."

All my life I thought I know God, until I finally opened the door

Phebe Atondo
Age: 13

AJ Kilmartin   Age 15
Bishop Bart is doing a great thing in the city.

Amira Mills
age 14
"God has changed me tremendously and its so unexplainable".

Chiebuka Ewuosic agrees that this is the generation under God. : years

Blaise Kilmartin
age 17

God is on the move in generation. He has called me, I have said yes and He is calling you too.

Anthony Nieves
Age: 17
"Advance the Kingdom"

Gabrielle Folson - 14
True love is real in God.

Atoryia, M'Allister   14

Prayer Changes Things.

Jordan Artis
Age: 16

compassion commission really helped me seek God everytime and give me a breakthrough.

Keiran, 13

"I couldnt do anything without god"

Mackenzie Ragitsingh
17 years old

I've decided to try my best to be obedient to God and what he is telling me.

Generation 3

The apostle Paul, in his letter to the church in Ephesus, used a particular phrase that still speaks loudly in the 21st-century church today: "every joint (generation) supplies." That is what this book, *The 5-G Shift,* is all about. Once in a while a book will come along that is written by divine inspiration that speaks to *everyone* all at the same time. This is one of those books. Bishop Bart Pierce, a proven, seasoned, apostolic voice has put together a multi-generational template that activates each one of us in whatever season or stage we are presently in. If you have had trouble discerning your season, look no further. You have now connected to a message that will bring clarity and alignment in your assignment for your days. *The 5-G Shift* will sift you (remove the wrong stuff), gift you (impart the right stuff), lift you (bring you up to your proper level), and finally, shift you (put you in position to accomplish the mission).

—Patrick D. Kiteley

Generation 4

Bishop Bart Pierce Has written another timely book based on his vast experience as a pastor, disciple maker, and city transformer. In this work he skillfully combines his keen prophetic foresight, biblical insight, and practical application that coalescences into an urgent call to the church to reach all five generations attending our church and beyond. A must read—I highly recommend it!

— Joseph Mattera
national convener for the
United States Coalition of Apostolic Leaders
Generation 4

Generation 5

Bart Pierce has written, not just a good book but an outstanding and amazing book. If you feel you have a hopeless life and no future, this is your book. If you have a church filled with confusion and suffering from many problems, and you don't know what to do to bring it back to the purposes of God, this is your book.

When you finish this book, you will realize a "miracle man" wrote it. You will find a man who many people gave up on—and finally, he almost gave up on himself. Then a merciful and loving God found him, saved him and filled him with the power of the Holy Spirit. Nothing was ever the same. All of the ministry gifts revealed by Paul the Apostle in Ephesians 4—Apostle, Prophet, Evangelist, Pastor and Teacher—have at one time or another been demonstrated in the life of this godly man.

If you start reading this book in the morning, a lot of your work for that day will not get done. If you start reading the book at night, you will lose a lot of sleep. I read it in one day. I have read thousands of books in my lifetime but never one like this. Whatever you do, get started on *The 5-G Shift* as soon as possible. I laid my hands on Bart Pierce when he was a youth leader in a local church and told him he would be known by and preach to millions of people. It happened.

—Dr. Charles Green—Bart Pierce's Spiritual Father
(who is very proud of his son)
New Orleans, Louisiana and Dallas, Texas

As communications in the IT world shift into the 5G realm, apostolic leader Bart Pierce prophetically explains the "5-G Shift" revelation for the Church of today and tomorrow. Pierce shares biblical insights and ministerial experiences as one who has walked many years in all of the 5-fold ministry gifts. This an extremely well balanced book—a must-read for all believers called to the work of the ministry.

—Dr. John P. Kelly
International Convenor of ICAL, (International
Coalition of Apostolic Leaders)

Introduction

O VER FORTY YEARS ago at a pastor's conference in Virginia Beach, Virginia, I was called
out of the crowd of over one hundred pastors
and leaders. This very intense woman, whose name
was Violet Kiteley, was preparing to speak to us. She
stopped, turned around and walked straight toward
me. Violet was pastoring a church in Oakland, California, and she had a reputation for being very accu-
rate in her prophetic words.

As a young girl growing up in Canada, she had wit-
nessed the powerful healing ministry of a man named
Smith Wigglesworth who would stay at her parents'
home when he was traveling through Canada. On one
of his trips, the neighbor's wife had died and was laid
on the kitchen table. The family asked Wigglesworth
to come over and pray.

As a young girl, Violet went with her parents and
this great man of God to the home of the dead woman. When they arrived at the home, Wigglesworth
went to the woman, who had been dead for a long
time. He lifted her up, pressed her dead, limp body

against a wall and prayed over her. When he finished praying, Sister Kiteley and those present stood in total amazement as the woman gasped and came back to life.

Sister Kiteley had also been a part of the Latter Rain Revival in Saskatchewan, Canada, when God showed up in 1948. Now, this small-framed but very intense woman was heading my way. She pointed at me and said, "Get your wife." My first thought was how she knew I was married. She couldn't see my hands to see my wedding ring.

She began to prophesy to me that my suitcases were packed and in the trunk of my car and that I was to unpack them and stay there at my home church because God was going to use me as the youth pastor. (We didn't have a youth pastor at our church at the time.) She said that God was going to put a rainbow of His covenant favor over my head and that whatever I asked of Him for the youth, God would grant my request.

From that point forward God began to orchestrate divine encounters with men and women of God from every area of ministry to impart, what I call "transpneumigration." (The transferring of anointing from one person to another.) One after another, more encounters like this began to happen.

I've come to refer to this as the silver cord of redemption, connecting my life as a Generation 2 at the time (12-25 years old) with powerful Generation 3s (25-50 years old) and 4s (50-70 years old). The 4s were the generation that had been in the presence of God and were carriers of His divine anointing with the intent to transfer it to young men and women like my wife and me.

The first encounter was while I was in Bible school at our home church, where we saw many great men and women of God come through to minister. One of our teachers, Dr. McKeown, was an older man (of Generation 5—70s plus). In the course of his teaching, he would often make reference to the presence of God. At these times, I noticed something would come over him, and it seemed he was having a deep encounter with God in that moment. Often, his eyes would well up with tears as he was overwhelmed with emotion.

One day after class I asked if I could speak with him, and he agreed to give me a few moments. In his Welsh accent he invited me to have a seat in his small office, and I went straight to the point.

"What happens to you when you start talking about the manifest presence of God?" I asked.

He looked at me almost as though he was sizing me up to see if I was really serious. Then he blew me away with a story of his mother taking him to a church on a weeknight in Wales where a young man told a testimony of his encounter with Jesus. The speaker's name was Evan Roberts, a man who history records as one of the main people God used to start and carry the great Welch revival in the early 1900s. I jumped up and asked Dr. McKeown to please pray for me, not wanting the moment to pass without this great man of God imparting to me what was on him from that encounter with God back in Wales.

Then, Violet Kiteley invited me to Oakland to be at a conference with college students. She took my hand and used it while she prayed for almost every one of these students and gave them each a powerful prophetic word. When she took me back to my hotel room, I couldn't sleep. I prayed in the spirit through the night, and my life would never be the same. Today, I move in the prophetic around the world from conferences of church people to heads of nations to marketplace ministers.

In 1975 I met a man from Southern California named David Schoch. He was at our church in Virginia Beach to minister, and there was a special leadership meeting with a presbytery for young couples who had a call of God in their lives. Along with Pastor Schoch was Dr. Charles Green, pastor of Word of Faith Church in New Orleans, who became one of my dearest friends and who is my pastor today. They prayed over my wife and me and defined our ministries in detail—even describing what we are engaged in today.

Pastor Schoch would later tell me the story of when, as a young man in Southern California, a great revivalist named John G. Lake had come to his home by a divine leading of God. Lake was in a communion meeting, along with eleven other ministers of the time, in Schoch's parents' home. Jesus showed up and ministered to these great men of God. I wanted what John G. Lake had deposited on Pastor Schoch. So, he was more than willing to lay hands on me and impart God's anointing.

This book is the prophetic mandate of the Lord to all of us who are 3s, 4s and even 5s—to turn around and reach back to Generations 1 and 2 and impart to them what Jesus has done for us and leave the mantle of anointing with these young men and women behind us

If we don't do this, we will be guilty of the sin described in Judges 2:10, in which Scripture says that the generation failed to transfer to the generations behind it all the great things God did for Israel when He brought them into the Promised Land. This is our last chance to allow the generation of 4s and 5s—who are still alive—to leave a spiritual legacy to the generation that follows them.

Billy Graham, Oral Roberts and many of our recent great spiritual leaders have gone on. So often there has not been that "transpneumigration" deposit to the next apostles, prophets, evangelists, pastors and teachers, to guarantee that the message of the Gospel will continue to take the church into the next great outpouring that is coming. Acts 2:39 is our clarion call to this next generation of Gen Xers, Millennials, Ys and Zs.

Enjoy this book, and then transfer what God has done for you to the next Kingdom nation changers.

chapter 1

Transpneumigration

I believe the future of Christianity, and the reformation that God will use to bring a shift in the church—and a shift in the culture—lies within the revelation of generational thinking.

MY WIFE THOUGHT I was dead. I was a 22-year-old surfer, high on LSD,[1] riding 25-mile-an-hour waves as high as buildings. *Crash!* A big wave hit, and I wiped out. She didn't see me anymore. When you're surfing like that, nothing but life or death is ahead of you. I wasn't sure what I was doing, but I didn't care—I had nothing to live for.

The lifestyle in the 60s went after extremes; and to me, the church represented the opposite—a weak, half-baked, unsanctified place that was fake and phony. I didn't know how wrong I was. I was about to be shocked by a church that saved my life and taught me how to be a disciple of Jesus.

---

1. LSD (Lysergic acid diethylamide).

I grew up in the streets, and I knew how to fight. My nickname was "Black Bart," because I was a drug dealer who was wanted up and down the East Coast. When I was nine years old, my mother died suddenly. After that, I just went crazy. In fifth grade, I was thrown out of school because I punched the principal in the stomach. In eighth grade, my teacher, Mr. Hendricks, grabbed me by the seat of the pants and threw me out the door. He told the principal, "If you bring him back in my class, I'll quit teaching school."

I was crazy: *Loco en la cabeza.*

By the time I was 13, I was in prison, and from then on I was in and out of jail. I always got in fights, which I never lost, with the exception of one. (I don't remember what happened, because I woke up after it was over.) Once, I jumped into a car with three guys inside and whipped them all. Another time, someone put a gun to my head and pulled the trigger, but he hit the sign above my head instead. When it was time to graduate high school, my principal wrote my stepmother a letter, which said, "If you will keep your son home from the graduation ceremony, we'll send him a certificate."

I lived on the East Coast oceanfront, and traveled all over the world as a pro surfer. Back then, if you won, they simply gave you T-shirts and surfboards—no money. My dad took me to construction sites and taught me the building trade, but he couldn't give me what I needed most: Jesus Christ. When I was 17, he choked on a piece of food and dropped dead in our kitchen. Just like that, one more positive influence was gone from my life.

If prayers and miracles hadn't been at work in my life, I wouldn't be alive in God today. Would you believe that I became a pastor, and started scores of Christian ministries—Including a Christian school? One day, I stood up and told the parents at our school about my background. They asked me incredulously, "Do you think I'm gonna put my kid in your school?" They couldn't believe it!

God had to do something radical to change my life— and He did. When the Jesus Movement broke out, a crazy evangelist named John Gimenez came to the Virginia Beach oceanfront, on the lookout for people like me. That day, I walked into Rock Church, with drugs in both pockets, and I got saved. I *really* got saved: nobody had to tell me I was. I knew I was born again. I had walked into one of the fastest-growing churches in America. Rock Church was exploding in every sense of the word. Hippies were coming in by the droves. I had been bound for hell; but instead, I went into a church and prayed, "Jesus, if you're real, come into my life." About ten other men stood up with me and prayed that same prayer. Afterwards, I said, "That was cool, man." I felt something. The next week, I told my wife, "Let's go again!" And then I caught on: this was it for me. I was in.

Evangelism got us in the door, but discipleship made us into people of God who loved and served Him with our lives. This vision of discipleship is what every local church needs. The local church is a microcosm of the universal church (the Body of Christ). We hippies were a wild bunch, but the local church didn't turn us away—just the opposite. They came looking for us, welcomed us in, and sat us down to be discipled and schooled in the Bible, until all we wanted was to become preachers ourselves.

From the pulpit, we looked like a wild, unfocused, intense, undisciplined, and unkempt group of young people. I remember the day Bob Mumford came to preach. When he saw us, he said to Brother John privately, "I'm intimidated by this group." The girls had hairy armpits and legs. Nobody wore underwear, bras, and things like that. Our blue jeans had holes in them—not because we bought them that way, but because they were worn out. The guys had long hair and goatees and bib overalls with no shirts. We filled the front rows of the church.

Brother John told Bob, "Don't worry—they're harmless! Just don't drop the microphone, because one of those fools will pick it up and preach!"

Today's millennial generation is drawn to extremes in ways that remind me of my generation long ago. Both groups yearned for something real—full of excitement and power. We found it in the church! We came in the door as hippies, and they sent us out as men and women of God. They taught us to put on the whole armor of God. Everybody preached that message to us. I heard hundreds of messages on it, because they knew we needed it.

The church needs something fresh. We need leaders who carry the presence of God, and also impart it to the younger generation—regardless of how they look. The local church is the only place that can make this whole process happen—feeding, counseling, protecting, and equipping the sheep—His body—to become a family of God that disciples nations.

Regardless of how we looked, the pastors knew we were hungry for reality. They told us people could be raised from the dead, so we were looking for it. They told us blind eyes could be opened, so we prayed for it. We laid hands on the blind, peeking the whole time to see their eyes get healed. Everything they told us was in the Bible, and we believed it.

They also introduced us to other ministers who were bold carriers of God's ark. These people had the same fire, the same wind, and the same power as the first disciples 2,000 years ago. It didn't seem to us any different than what we read in the Book of Acts. I remember when R. W. Shambach came to Rock Church. His voice thundered and shook like a wind tunnel. People came from all over to hear him. We saw people get slain in the

Spirit, and we were right there catching them. We didn't know it, but during that time, his spirit was being transferred to us.

T. L. Osborne came in, and Winston Nunes. Myrtle "Mom" Beall came from Bethesda Missionary Temple in Detroit. One day, Mom Beale grabbed my arm. I thought I'd been electrocuted. Power came out of her mouth when she spoke. Then, Violet Kiteley came and turned my world upside down. I was sitting onstage with about 75 preachers. She pointed her finger at me and called me out. She told me to get my wife and said, "Your suitcases are in the back of your car. Unpack them. You're not going."

We found new pathways to God through these people. A silver cord was invisibly sewing us together. Before God sews something, He looks for a certain fabric—an instrument He can use to thread the needle. Then, He sews us together as the Church, and we become a unified garment He can use for His glory.

When I got saved, I asked, "God, could you use me?" I had no idea what I was saying. I'd never been in church; I didn't know how to read the Bible. (I didn't even have one.) But I said, "God, here I am." I am so glad that, somehow, I had enough wherewithal to say, "Here's my life." I have no regrets. I'd rather do what I'm doing for Jesus than anything else I could have done with my life before I met Him. I could have been an attorney. I had the opportunity to be climb the ladder in construction. But this is the best of the best!

I have pastored Rock City Church in Baltimore, Maryland, for 35 years. I am still convinced that the local church is the best place for transformation in any person's life. Discipleship directed by a local pastor is the best way to shape the character of young lives, because only the church can build the best kind of character—the character of Christ-likeness. The local church is also the only place where people work consistently and sacrificially to serve and rescue others throughout their lives.

Every year, our local church performs a play called "From Here to Eternity." All the actors and the production team are volunteers from our church. Our members produce the sound, lighting, props, and every other aspect of the performance. Our people are totally committed and really look forward to doing this play every year. They are willing to sacrifice. They are sewn together with a silver cord. They are established on the foundation of our local church.

Over the past 20 years, more than 135,000 people have attended this performance at Rock City Church. One year, the police had to shut down the beltway near our exit because 4,000 people were inside the church and another 4,000 more were backed up on the highway, clogging streets, trying to get here. Every year, after the play ends, kids rush down to the altar to get saved.

We have seen 500 to 600 kids get saved, weeping and crying. Some were going to commit suicide; some were on drugs; some were just hopeless and didn't know what to do. The power of God dropped in and touched those kids. Thousands came to Christ over the years.

When I first came to Rock City Church 35 years ago, I had no vision for this. John Gimenez actually sent me here to shut down the church because it had gone through a bad period and was falling apart. Even the buildings were affected. If you touched the ceiling, stuff fell down on your head. Pipes were hanging. It was smelly and dingy. There were only a handful of people attending, and the worst music you ever heard was played in our services.

While I was preaching to this small group, all of a sudden, the Holy Ghost came on me. I started prophesying the opposite of what I was seeing. I said, "God's going to make this a great church! This church will be used all over the world!" When I finished, I said, "That was either the stupidest thing I've ever done, or somebody else is coming up here, not me." To make a long story short, I *did* end up being the one to come to Rock City Church—my wife and I moved to Baltimore, and we are still here.

It's Time for a Transfer of Spirit—Transpneumigration

How does a dying local church become a great church? Only God can do it, and He did it for us. Praise the Lord!

The goal of the Holy Spirit is to sovereignly bring the universal church back to God's intended pattern, which is to cover the earth with the knowledge of His glory and disciple nations, as Jesus said in Matthew 28:19-20. That work begins in the local church, where God empowers pastors and leaders of the five-fold ministry to produce people who arise and impact nations.

In order to be successful, every local church needs to practice a transfer of anointing—a transfer of spirit—from the shepherd (leader) to the sheep (disciples). The Greek word for a transfer of spirit is "transpneumigration." This word is made up of the words *trans*—to move (from one place to another), *pneuma*—spirit, and *migration,* which means to establish a new residence in a new place.

I'd received a transfer of spirit by transpneumigration before I was sent to Baltimore to face that dead church. My pastor, John Gimenez, was not afraid of death. He defied it. One time, when a man dropped dead at Rock Church, the rescue squad came and pronounced him dead. However, Brother John went to the back pew where the man was laying and laid his hands on him, saying, "You get up! You're not dying in my church! I don't want the testimony that a man died in my church!" The man came back to life and got up off the pew!

After God gave me the prophetic word that this dead church would come back to life, I had faith to believe

I could bring it back to life. I believed that I could lay hands on that church, and they would receive the Holy Ghost through me. There are biblical models for this. The apostles sent Peter and John to a weak church in Samaria that heard the Word of God but had no power of the Holy Ghost. Peter and John were carriers of the Holy Ghost; they went and laid hands on the church. That was transpneumigration—the transfer of a life-giving spirit to the church through those men.

> *Now when the apostles which were at Jerusalem heard that Samaria had received the word of God, they sent unto them Peter and John: Who, when they were come down, prayed for them, that they might receive the Holy Ghost: (For as yet he was fallen upon none of them: only they were baptized in the name of the Lord Jesus.) Then laid they their hands on them, and they received the Holy Ghost. (Acts 8:14-17, KJV)*

When Jesus ministered to people, the Holy Spirit passed through His hands. Now, the Spirit passes through the hands of men like Peter and John, and you and me. The Holy Spirit can be transferred by the laying on of hands, in which people receive the Holy Ghost and power.

Many churches today are weak because they are just *playing* church. They have no Holy Ghost power; they have no fresh insight from God; they haven't changed anything substantial for years. Change doesn't mean adding big screens and flashing lights to the Sunday service; I'm talking about finding out what God sees in your soul, and changing anything that is not like Him.

Here's What Happened in My Church—The 5-G Shift

One of the most alarming shortcomings in today's churches is a lack of commitment to the younger generation. Older generations have their tickets punched and are on their way to heaven. Middle generations are consumers who come to church for a good word before they go to dinner and eat too much. No one seems to be investing in the future the way God sees it.

Statistics say the American church is declining; but not Rock City Church. Families here are doing well. Children grow up and go away college, but come back and take responsibilities in the church. The police depend on us to work with youth in the inner city. We build houses for the poor. We stand publicly against anything contrary to God's Word, and we create programs to back our stands. We oppose abortion, so we support pregnant women and help them keep their babies after they're born. We've saved a thousand babies so far.

One of the most radical things I've done in recent years was fire the youth minister—not on the basis of anything he did, but on principle. In most churches, including ours, the youth ministry becomes a babysitting service; however, God wants a generational transfer from father to children, both in the home and in the church. After I fired the youth pastor, I gave back to our parents the responsibility for their children's spiritual development. They could teach them at home and also bring them to church services.

The church in America needs a generational shift. There are 5 generations alive today, so I call this shift a 5-G Shift.

Generation 1—Conception to age 12

Generation 2—Ages 12 to 25

Generation 3—Ages 25-50

Generation 4—Ages 50-70

Generation 5—Over 70

The older generations—G3, G4, and G5—in many cases have been living for themselves. According to the Bible, they should turn to their children and direct them on the right path. When this happens, I believe we will have a revolution in about *six months*.

The first time I introduced this generational concept at Rock City Church, something happened spontaneously: people wanted to wash one another's feet. Some went looking for buckets and put water in them; others found towels. The older generations washed the feet of the younger and said, "It's time that our generation comes back." The G2s washed the feet of the G1s. Everybody was crying.

Jesus, the greater, knelt down and washed the feet of the lesser (John 13). When the G2s, the greaters, washed the feet of the lesser G1s, the G1s saw their humility and wanted to be just like them.

Behold, I will send you Elijah the prophet before the coming of the great and dreadful day of the LORD: And he shall turn the heart of the fathers to the children, and the heart of the children to their fathers, lest I come and smite the earth with a curse. (Malachi 4:5-6, KJV)

When the church starts the 5- G Shift, things will begin to change in the church that will affect society. God can begin to bring revival in our midst! I'm not here to play church. These are serious times. We can't live on some-body else's dream, or somebody else's move of God. It's time to move forward aggressively in God, using all of the weapons of warfare He has given us for today!

chapter 2

Spiritual Fathers

*In the next year, the technology of 5G (5th Generation) cell
phone technology will bring a revolutionary shift in our ability
to communicate and process data. When you read a 5G news
story in the days to come, remember the 5-G Shift that's needed
in the church. Pray about your role in the coming restoration.
The church today is not ready for rulership, dominion, or any
of the visionary things we've preached for the past 20 years.
The church is asleep in Zion, and not mature enough to handle
leadership. But God always has a remnant. This time, the
remnant needs to bring a 5-G Shift to the church.*

A FATHER IN OUR church in Baltimore, who comes
from Nigeria, arrived home from work one day
to find his son dead in the yard. His boy had been
with us since he was born. He'd been executed—shot in
the back. The killers laid him out with his feet together and his baseball cap on top of his feet with his hands
crossed. The detective told us that, when drug dealers
pose kids like that, they're saying, "Don't you mess with
us, and don't you tell anybody. We know where you live."

I get calls to bury inner city kids so often that I have to work with two funeral homes in Baltimore who perform services for free. We bury kids all the time. I'm tired of burying kids.

If you ask G2 kids in the streets of Baltimore how long they think they'll live, most of them will tell you, "If I live to be 21 or 22, I've made it." Most of them don't believe they're going to live past 22 years old. They have a fatalistic approach because they have no hope in God. They have no sense that there's a God protecting them, let alone a God who gives their lives purpose and meaning.

Drug dealers and members of murderous gangs usually grow up without fathers. They have no natural fathers, and they have no spiritual fathers. They don't know God as their heavenly Father, so they invent their own gods in their own images. These guys are violent, angry, lost, and at their wits' end. They may never know Jesus Christ—unless God changes us in the church and we grow up.

Why is the church so weak today? The answer is because people come to church when they feel like it—if it fits into their schedule (wherein the calendar week starts on Monday instead of Sunday, to reflect their true priorities). They have lost the vision for prayer, so they give the job to intercessors. Prayer over a meal is about all you get, if that. They don't read the Bible because they have left that up to the preacher. They make decisions independently, as if it doesn't matter to God and He doesn't care or know what they do. So much compromise is built into their lives that it creates a constant downward spiral; yet they still expect to go to heaven.

If we keep doing church this way, we will keep putting empty heads in empty buildings. We will lose the younger generations. The Bible says that the sons of Issachar were "men who had understanding of the times to know what Israel ought to do" (1 Chronicles 12:32, AMPC). Churches need to wake up and understand the times—the season in which we're living. Christians need to know what they ought to do and stop making excuses. We must do the work of God in our generation, until God says we are finished.

Inner City Revival

Inner cities need revival, and they'll see it when the power of God falls on G2 kids—when they stop killing one another and get saved. Then, these saved kids will go to somebody who has been shot dead, lay hands on them, and God will restore the dead to life. Then you will see revival.

A young man in my church named Rick, whom I led to Jesus, was on his way to perform at an event we were holding. He stopped at a grocery store to buy something, dressed in a costume that looked like a can. While he was in the back of the store, he saw a guy with a gun holding up the woman at the cash register. Rick went forward, yelling, "Hey, you can't do this!"

The robber shot at him, but his gun jammed. Rick kept coming, bouncing along in his can costume. Rick yelled again, "Hey, you! Stop that! Get out of here!" The guy robbing the store was getting nervous as Rick came toward him, but he shot again. This time, the gun went off. Somehow, the bullet went into a hamburger in the glass case behind Rick. Nobody could figure out later how the bullet circled around him like that.

A broadcast went out over the police radio: "A man just robbed the Giant grocery store, and another man is chasing him wearing a suit that looks like a can!" The guy was running down the street as fast as he could, and Rick was running after him. A robber with a gun ran away from a Christian, even though he looked like a can, because he carried the power of God.

The power of God is referred to in the Bible with the Greek word *dunamis*. When we older generations transfer our spirits to the G2s and G1s, as we are supposed to do, they will have *dunamis*. They will have power. They will become the guardians of the streets. They will become the guardians of their schools. Instead of girls getting raped in school bathrooms, Christian kids will have the power and protection of God against the devil. Supernatural things will begin to happen.

Churches today are too often led by immature men and women who act more like babysitters than generals. They can't handle the pressure of real ministry, as God defines it. They are too immature. Immaturity has nothing to do with chronological age. I've seen 80-year-olds who acted like fools. I've seen 16-year-olds who needed a pacifier, and I've seen 15-year-olds who acted like men and women, because they knew they had a call of God on their lives.

Babysitter pastors don't have Jesus' vision for the church—to see the Body of Christ as a force for change that "the gates of hell shall not prevail against" (Matthew 16:18, KJV). When parents hire babysitters, they don't expect them to have vision for their children's spiritual lives. They are only hired to occupy the children while the parents are away. Babysitters in the church have no true vision for the future of their people and the role that these people are to play in the kingdom. They only occupy time on Sundays with religious entertainment, while the those they should be converting and developing spiritually are perishing.

Where there is no vision, the people perish. (Proverbs 29:18, KJV)

Every father with a vision for his family makes daily investments in his children's lives. Likewise, a pastor is to make a spiritual investment in his sons and daughters in the church. Otherwise, he is just an instructor. Paul explained the significance of a spiritual father and gave himself as an example:

For though ye have ten thousand instructors in Christ, yet have ye not many fathers: for in Christ Jesus I have begotten you through the gospel. (1 Corinthians 4:15, KJV)

The Greek word for "instructors" means "boy leader." A pastor who makes no spiritual investment is a boy leader in his church. The church in Corinth was probably the first megachurch: it had a thousand instructors; however, Paul warned the Corinthians not to overlook their responsibility to make an investment as spiritual fathers. He looked at them and said, "You do not have many fathers."

The church needs spiritual fathers who add the strength of steel to the church's infrastructure so that it can build on what God wants it to do. Look what the author of Hebrews has to say about this topic:

Therefore, leaving the principles of the doctrine of Christ, let us go on unto perfection. (Hebrews 6:1, NASB)

When the Bible says to go on to perfection, this means full-grown maturity—fullness of growth. This phrase relates to the union between learning and practicing. I tell people all the time that I'm a practitioner; I'm not a theorist. A lot of people are stuck in learning, and they never move on to practicing the lifestyle of a mature Christian.

People come to church on Sunday and hear a repetition of the same thing they've heard before. We should all pray. *(Hallelujah.)* We should all fast. *(Hallelujah.)* We should all worship. *(Hallelujah.)* We should all read our Bibles. *(Hallelujah.)* Pastors repeat and repeat and repeat; but God doesn't want them to get stuck there. They need to go on! It's time to grow up and practice what we have learned! The evidence of perfection in your walk with God is revealed in how you practice the elements of what you've learned. You are no longer a child. You are a parent taking responsibility for others' growth. You are active, not passive.

Instructors in Paul's day were hired servants, like nannies. They were young boys who made sure others' children went to school and were held accountable. In recent years, too many pastors have become like nannies with no spiritual interest in those they watch over. They refuse to move past the outward traditions of a Sunday service—these are passive, milquetoast, compromising pastors who want to please everybody except God. As a result, the Gospel is made of no effect. As Mark puts it, they are "Making the word of God of none effect through your tradition" (Mark 7:13, KJV).

Transpneumigration

The church moves forward through a generational transfer of spirit—transpneumigration. I am a product of a transfer of spirit. Thank God my church had lots of G3s and G4s when we came in as G2s. The G3s and G4s gave up everything for me as a young G2 Christian so that I could mature, discover my identity in Christ, and become what I am today. The Jesus Movement brought together a great gathering of preachers and ministers—who are still in practice!

I thank God that, after I got saved and started learning, I was encouraged to practice what I learned. Older generations sacrificed to give us what they had to ensure that we could grow up in God. They gave up their front-row seats in the church and moved to the back so hundreds of us hippies could sit in the front of the House of God.

They gave up their jobs; they gave up their money to invest in us. The first suit I ever owned came from a G4 spiritual father at Rock Church who bought me the suit, a sport jacket, two ties, and two sets of shirts and pants. When I went to church in my new suit, John Gimenez said, "Bart, come up here and testify." While I was talking to the church, I got so overwhelmed by the presence of the Holy Spirit that I blurted out everything. I said, "Isn't it amazing that God let the very man that I stole milk from buy me my first suit?" His wife's eyes got as big as saucers. She turned to him and asked,

"You bought him a suit, and he stole our milk?" God has a great sense of humor.

If you are in my church today, I'm your spiritual father. It's irrelevant whether you were born again in my church or in somebody else's church. When you're in my church, you are my responsibility. I have to help you grow up spiritually and stop being a baby. I work hard to bring you from your new spiritual birth to full maturity in Christ.

Paul had an issue with the Corinthian church because of its boy leaders; however, boy leaders are allowed to pastor churches today. They are placed in leadership before they mature—before they've been tested and proven; before they've developed spiritual authority and power through trials. Other pastors begin churches on the basis of rebellion against senior leadership. These pastors start their own church and produce Ishmaels. When immature men rule, Isaiah says, that is a judgment from God. Those leaders don't know how to develop people and make them grow up into their destiny. They accommodate them in their weaknesses and adapt their Sunday messages to their babyhood.

When the church is weak, the nation is weak. People move away from God. The result is oppression.

I will give children to be their princes, and babes shall rule over them. And the people shall be oppressed, every one by another, and every one by his neighbor: the child shall behave himself proudly against the ancient. (Isaiah 3:4-5, KJV)

Immature leaders disrespect their elders. When Isaiah says "the child shall behave himself proudly against the ancient," it means the children are too proud to submit to those with gray hair—those with maturity who can help them grow up.

The Example of the Sons of Jehonadab

Jeremiah tells a great story in the Old Testament about honoring elders. He tells how the sons of Jehonadab son of Rechab honored the senior leadership of their family line, and each generation continued to keep their ancestors' commitments to God that had been passed down to them. In Jeremiah 35:1-16, he writes:

This is the message the LORD gave Jeremiah when Jehoiakim son of Josiah was king of Judah:

"Go to the settlement where the families of the Rechabites live, and invite them to the LORD's Temple. Take them into one of the inner rooms, and offer them some wine."

So I went to see Jaazaniah son of Jeremiah and grandson of Habazziniah and all his brothers and sons—representing all the Rechabite families. I took them to the Temple, and we went into the room. . . .

I set cups and jugs of wine before them and invited them to have a drink, but they refused. "No," they said, "we don't drink wine, because our ancestor Jehonadab son of Rechab gave us this command: 'You and your descendants must never drink wine. And do not build houses or plant crops or vineyards, but always live in tents. If you follow these commands, you will live long, good lives in the land.' **So we have obeyed him in all these things.** We have never had a drink of wine to this day, nor have our wives, our sons, or our daughters. We haven't built houses or owned vineyards or farms or planted crops. We have lived in tents and have fully obeyed all the commands of Jehonadab, our ancestor. But when King Nebuchadnezzar of Babylon attacked this country, we were afraid of the Babylonian and Syrian armies. So we decided to move to Jerusalem. That is why we are here."

Then the Lord gave this message to Jeremiah:

"This is what the Lord of Heaven's Armies, the God of Israel, says: 'Go and say to the people in Judah and Jerusalem, "Come and learn a lesson about how to obey me. The Rechabites do not drink wine to this *day because their ancestor Jehonadab told them not to. But I have spoken to you again and again, and you refuse to obey me. Time after time I sent you prophets, who told you, 'Turn from your wicked ways, and start doing things right. Stop worshiping other gods so that you might live in peace here in the land I have given to you and your ancestors.' But you would not listen to me or obey me. **The descendants of Jehonadab son of Rechab have obeyed their ancestor completely, but you have refused to listen to me.'''** (NLT, emphasis added)*

Notice how this group of children honored the vows of their spiritual father—their ancestor, Jehonadab son of Rechab—throughout succeeding generations. Their obedience to their vows continued from their father's generation to the present one. Even God was impressed—He said, "Because you have obeyed the command . . . he shall not lack a man to stand before me all of your days." This was a generational blessing.

Deuteronomy 5:9 says that sin is passed down to the third and fourth generations: "I, the LORD your God, am a jealous God, visiting the iniquity of the fathers on the children, and on the third and the fourth generations of those who hate Me" (KJV). However, by the grace of God, His blessings are passed down to a thousand generations of those who love Him: ". . . showing love to a thousand generations of those who love me and keep my commandments" (Deuteronomy 5:10, NIV). God's blessings will only come, and the church and culture will only change, when G3 and G4 fathers repent and say, "I'm sorry. I've been selfish. I've wanted to be blessed myself. I will turn now, and bless the generations behind me."

Jesus said that those coming behind Him would do greater works than He had done. The volume of great things Jesus had done would be multiplied because He had transferred His spirit to those coming after Him.

Jesus said, "Truly, truly, I say to you, he who believes in Me, the works that I do, he will do also; and greater works than these he will do; because I go to the Father." (John 14:12, NASB)

Listen to me, G3 and G4 dads: it's up to us. We've got to repent and invest in our G2 and G1 sons and daughters! One of the biggest hindrances today is the broken connection in father-child relationships.

Jesus told a parable about a father with an unbroken connection to his son through unconditional love. In Jesus' parable of the Prodigal Son, the boy leaves his father and ends up working with pigs. A Jewish boy should not have been around pigs; he should not have been eating with pigs. That was totally against their culture. But the prodigal son was far away from God, and he had walked away from his father, who could have taught him the things of God. The Bible says that finally the boy came to himself:

And when he came to himself, he said, How many hired servants of my father's have bread enough and to spare, and I perish with hunger! (Luke 15:17, KJV)

You have to come to yourself before you can come to God. If you don't deal with your "self," your self will take you away from God. Jesus said that, when the Prodigal was near his home, his father saw his son from afar off. In other words, the father saw the son in the spirit before he saw him in the flesh. God the Father sees you before you come to Him. He always sees you. You can't hide from your Father.

And there is no creature hidden from His sight, but all things are open and laid bare to the eyes of Him with whom we have to do. (Hebrews 4:13, NASB)

God sees the beginning and the end; and He sees the end from the beginning. God gave Jeremiah a remarkable understanding of how He saw him before he was even born, and called him to be a prophet while he was still in his mother's womb.

Now the word of the LORD came to me saying, "Before I formed you in the womb I knew you, and before you were born I consecrated you; I have appointed you a prophet to the nations." (Jeremiah 1:4-5, NASB)

Jesus also saw Nathanael before he came to Him to be a disciple: "Nathanael said to Him, 'How do You know me?' Jesus answered and said to him, 'Before Philip called you, when you were under the fig tree, I saw you'" (John 1:48, NASB).

Before Jesus came, the last prophetic words God would utter for about 400 years are found in the book of Malachi. This was written during a period of time when things were changing. Look at what God says:

Behold, I will send you Elijah the prophet before the great and terrible day of the Lord comes. And he shall turn and reconcile the hearts of the [estranged] fathers to the [ungodly] children, and the hearts of the [rebellious] children to [the piety of] their fathers [a reconciliation produced by repentance of the ungodly], lest I come and smite the land with a curse and a ban of utter destruction. (Malachi 4:5-6, AMPC)

This prophecy is confirmed in Luke 1:17, where it says that John the Baptist would come in the spirit and the power of Elijah, in order to turn the hearts of the fathers to the children:

It is he who will go as a forerunner before Him in the spirit and power of Elijah, It is he who will go as a forerunner before Him in the spirit and power of Elijah, TO TURN THE HEARTS OF THE FATHERS BACK TO THE CHILDREN, *and the disobedient to the attitude of the righteous, so as to make ready a people prepared for the Lord. (Luke 1:17, NASB)*

So we have two accounts—one in the Old Testament, and one in the New Testament, the latter coming on the heels of a period wherein God had been quiet. God says in Malachi, "I'm going to send the spirit of Elijah." Then He says in Luke, "I'm going to send the spirit of Elijah," and He identifies how the spirit would come through a man born to Zacharias and Elizabeth: John the Baptist. This man would be radical prophet crying out for people to repent. John would turn the hearts of the fathers to the children.

Today, we need that same spirit. We need better parenting, both naturally and spiritually. If we have a reformation of thinking, we can bring the church into a place in which we'll pass on God's blessing for generations. We need to recognize the importance of each individual's role as a believer, and how each one—even the ghetto kids—fits into the big picture. This way, we'll become spiritual fathers who raise up sons and daughters to a maturity that practices what it believes.

The Bible says there will be immature people in the last days who will be lovers of self more than lovers of God:

"For men will be lovers of self, lovers of money, boastful, arrogant, revilers, disobedient to parents, ungrateful, unholy . . . Lovers of pleasure rather than lovers of God." (2 Timothy 3:2-4, NASB)

We live in this day right now. People think, "It's all about me. Everything is based on how I feel and what is happening to me. Me, me, me, me, me, me, me." Self-centeredness gets you stuck on sameness. Churches don't move forward. No one is rushing to the altar to get saved. They've spent all this time, energy, and money, but they've not made progress for years. They haven't moved forward in their influence on the world.

We need a shift—a 5-G Shift—to teach the generations behind us what it means to be a real Christian. We need to impart a new spirit through transpneumigration. When churches are stuck on sameness, it takes a move of God to get them unstuck. We may have to butt some heads. People say, "Hey, I've been doing this too long; I can't change now." They don't want to change, but they have no choice if the church is going to be restored to its destiny in God.

I was raised in a church environment filled with a supernatural expectation of change. I went to church never knowing what was coming next. In the Jesus Movement, we looked wild, but we were coming to church whether you liked it or not. The people who welcomed us were fearless parents. They welcomed our change. They knew God was moving on our hearts. We looked like we were from another planet; but we were what we were. We knew that we were desperate, and we found Christians willing to meet us where we were. We knew we needed something—we knew truth existed— and we found people willing to give us the truth, no matter what it cost them. Those were our spiritual fathers and mothers.

Now, I want to tell you more about our spiritual mothers. These women were no less awesome and inspiring than our fathers. They gave us everything they had to give and more, and we became the people we are today because of their sacrifices.

chapter 3

Spiritual Mothers

I *F YOU WERE* to ask Anne Gimenez of Rock Church
Ministerial Fellowship, she would tell you that, as
soon as I was saved, I brought in hundreds of crazy people like me from the streets and beaches. I knew
right away that this was a life-changing church with
spiritual fathers like Brother John and spiritual mothers like Sister Anne.

Pastors can't keep their distance from people who
look and act as we did. We needed them to be our spiritual fathers and mothers. We needed them to lay hands
on us and transfer their anointing through transpneumigration. The superstructure of a great kingdom
church is built upon the Logos—the Word of God—and
transformed lives. Churches need the principles of the
doctrine of Christ, and they also need people who are
growing to spiritual maturity. Sometimes, that means
we need to bring strangers into our homes.

At Rock Church, we met a spiritual mother named Betty Forbes. Sister Betty came from a proper Methodist background, and you could tell from one look at her house. It was professionally furnished. Every Friday night, Betty opened her neat home to about 50 hippies like me with shaggy hair, dirty feet, and despicable jeans. We would pack into her house, drape over her French Provincial chairs, and sprawl out on her baby blue carpet. Most people would've said we were more suited for beanbags on a concrete floor, but Sister Betty never flinched. Her house was not too good for beach bums like us who'd found Jesus and wanted to grow in God.

One of the former druggies liked to play the piano. This guy would raise the cover on her beautiful, upright piano and start pounding the keys. Then, all of us would sing and shout until the house shook (and probably the neighborhood, too). It was the sound of newly saved people singing their hearts out to God. And God came down! Kids began weeping. People got healed. We were knocked to the floor and we would lie there for hours, worshipping the Lord, caught up in His glory.

When it was time to leave, we'd already been changed. We couldn't do enough to help Sister Betty move back the furniture and straighten the white doilies on her tables. Why? Because we were no longer dirty hippies. We were being transformed into future preachers by the love of a spiritual mother. We couldn't wait until next Friday.

Those Southern country folk who became our spiritual parents at Rock Church loved apple pie and Chevrolets, but they loved us more. They were not too good to invite renegades like us into their homes. As we grew in God, we became great friends with them, and continue to be today. Eventually, they sent us out to plant hundreds of churches and start ministries for drug addicts, homes for unwed mothers, prep schools for children (whether they could pay tuition or not), and Bible schools for pastors and foreign missionaries.

At Rock City Church in Baltimore, we opened a food warehouse. At the last count, we were feeding about 2,700 people a month, and it's still growing. We've also renovated and given away 18 houses so far in the inner city of Baltimore. Today's G2s and G1s need people who put their faith into practice and care about spiritual and natural needs. They need spiritual moms willing to teach them. However, the church has been asleep in Zion. Wake up, mothers! Wake up for the sake of the children!

God, I pray that you send revival to the young people through spiritual mothers in the older generations. Bring a new reformation, a new mindset, so that the culture will never again be able to extract God out of their lives.

A Demonic Mother's Lasting Influence

In the 1960s, shortly before we got saved and met Sister Anne and Sister Betty, there was another mother on the prowl in America—an ungodly mother. She had the opposite effect on children and youth. Her atheistic crusade to take God out of public education in Baltimore—the city where we would later plant Rock City Church—spread farther and lasted longer in American culture than the influence of the church. The changes she promoted in American public life still persist today, decades after she was murdered by her own demonic colleagues.

This crusading Baltimore mother was Madalyn Murray O'Hair (1919-1995). Her son, William J. "Bill" Murray III, was a public school student when she sued the Baltimore public school system on his behalf in a case that came to be called *Murray v. Curlett*. Madalyn claimed she and her son were atheists; therefore, it was unconstitutional for the school to require Bill to participate in morning exercises that included the Lord's Prayer and daily Bible reading, because that conflicted with Bill's beliefs.

Unitarians in Pennsylvania had filed another suit in a case called *Abington School District v. Schempp*. Soon *Murray v. Curlett* joined *Schempp*. On June 17, 1963, the U.S. Supreme Court ruled in their favor. The Court declared that sanctioned and organized Bible reading in public schools was unconstitutional.[2] God must be removed from the public schools.

My G4 generation took God out of the public schools. Then the G3 generation (today's 25-50 year olds) took God out of everything. Then the G2 generation inherited a society with no God, no fathers, no reverence for life (including their own) and confusion about everything. They now kill one another at a murderous pace in Baltimore, Chicago, Washington, Oakland, and other major cities—especially blacks-on-blacks—because they don't know who their fathers are, or who they are. They don't know if they're boys or girls. They kill themselves over social medial, and other kids would commit suicide if they had enough guts to do it.

"Whatever You Ask for the Youth, I Will Give It to You"
In the 1970s, the late Violet Kiteley, co-founder of Shiloh Church in Oakland, California, spoke this prophecy over me:

> *"Thus sayeth the Lord, I have placed a rainbow over your head, and whatever you ask for the youth, I will give it to you."*

Here is what I am asking from God for the youth—I am asking Him for a spiritual force willing to transfer their

2. School District of Abington Township, Pennsylvania v. Schempp. Online at *https://www.law.cornell.edu/supremecourt/text/374/203.* Accessed May 2019.

spirit to the G2 generation so that those G2s will go to the streets and universities of America and say, "Stop! I will not let that happen!" Right now, the universities and the rest of the world basically ignore the church. The Bible says that's because they can't hear us. They can't hear God. They have nonspiritual ears.

But the natural, nonspiritual man does not accept or welcome or admit into his heart the gifts and teachings and revelations of the Spirit of God, for they are folly (meaningless nonsense) to him; and he is incapable of knowing them [of progressively recognizing, understanding, and becoming better acquainted with them] because they are spiritually discerned and estimated and appreciated. (1 Corinthians 2:14, AMPC)

The world thinks the church is speaking "meaningless nonsense," but that's because their ears don't work correctly. We are speaking the truth, but they are spiritually deaf.

Jesus told us to disciple nations:

And Jesus came up and spoke to them, saying, "All authority has been given to Me in heaven and on earth. Go therefore and make disciples of all the nations, baptizing them in the name of the Father and the Son and the Holy Spirit, teaching them to observe all that I commanded you; and lo, I am with you always, even to the end of the age." (Matthew 28:18-20, NASB)

The youth of our nation, and every other nation, are being deceived. They need to be discipled by spiritual mothers and fathers so that they receive the truth. Today, most of what we do in the church is discipling one another. The same people come to church each week; the same discipleship class is repeated every year. We tell people the same things over and over. The older generations, G4 and G5, are satisfied. They are on their way to heaven. But God is not satisfied.

Discipleship now means that a woman calls her friend on the phone and listens to her complain about her bad day. Then she says, "Oh, I feel anointed. I'll pray for you. God is going to bless you." Then, three weeks later, she has to make the same call again. Three months later, she has to call again and go through the same routine, because women who should be spiritual mothers spend all of God's goodness on themselves.

A 5-G Shift can change that.

It's Time for a Bigger Earthquake

Scientists tell us that minor earthquakes are a common occurrence on earth, but most of them register below 3 or 4 on the Richter scale, so no one feels them.

That describes the church. We are barely causing a tremor. We can easily be ignored. We hardly register on the scale used by the world, and rarely cause damage to the powers of darkness. The church needs to create a bigger earthquake—with a 5-G generational shift.

The church should lead, and force the culture to catch up. Instead, natural, nonspiritual people are running things, moving in the opposite direction from God. They are running the industries. The 50-year-olds are running politics, but they don't have a prayer life. They don't even know Jesus exists. They would rather get drunk and have a cocktail party than go to church and worship the Lord. They think the church's teachings and revelations from the Spirit of God are folly and meaningless nonsense.

Earthquakes happen when tectonic plates move in opposite directions: "The movement of tectonic plates causes earthquakes when two plates that are in contact with each other move in opposite directions and release built-up stress. For example, one plate may move north, while the other may move south."[3] The church should be so opposite from the world that, when we confront one another, it creates an earthquake. Right now, the church is not moving in the opposite direction from the world. We go along with the culture, when God wants us be its opposite. We need a 5-G Shift. Then, He can send

3. How Does the Movement of Tectonic Plates Cause Earthquakes? Online at *https://www.reference.com/science/movement-tectonic-plates-cause-earthquakes-190da883030ad467.* Accessed May 1, 2019.

a spiritual earthquake. If the church in America would turn its heart towards G2s and G1s, you would see a spiritual earthquake in about six months.

As soon as the church moves in the opposite direction from the world, there will be such a shaking from the 5-G shift that people will be forced to acknowledge God. In this description of the largest historical earthquake in the continental United States (1812), notice that the shaking of the earth caused the ringing of church bells:

The largest known earthquake to hit the continental United States began near the town of New Madrid, Missouri, in 1812. It affected an area more than 10 times larger than the 1906 San Francisco earthquake— the shaking even rang church bells more than 1,000 miles away. The Mississippi River was thrown out of its channel and ran backwards for a time, and the terrain was so distorted that lifelong residents got lost on their own land.[4]

When was the last time that church bells rang spontaneously because there was such a great spiritual shift?

The G3 generation includes millennials; the world calls this age group "snowflakes," because they fall apart in a second. You can't say anything without offending them. Air offends them; water offends them. How did

---

4. "Earthquakes and Plates." Online at *https://oceanexplorer.noaa.gov/ edu/learning/1_plate_tectonics/activities/earthquakes_plates.html.* Accessed May 1, 2019.

this come to be? Some millennials served in the military in Iraq and Afghanistan. They learned how to go to war for their country, but they can't find spiritual warfare in the church. There are not enough spiritual mothers and fathers laying hands on them and teaching them how to wage war against the devil.

Every generation must teach spiritual warfare to the generation coming after them. Otherwise, the younger generations become subject to demonic spirits in the culture, with the same resulting defeats and denials of God that we've seen become commonplace. This will cease to be the case when the church makes a 5-G Shift. Millennials are no more of a challenge than my generation was back in the sixties. They simply need the love and impartation of spiritual mothers and fathers who will nurture them as they grow in God. They need our help to find out who they are in God, so they can throw off all the foolishness the world is throwing at them.

Spiritual parents in the church can stand in the gap generationally, but we must become willing to go all the way. When my G4 generation took prayer out of school in the sixties, there was still some sense of God-consciousness. We still knew that God existed. However, because there was no transpneumigration to the next generation, this knowledge of God declined. My generation left no strict instructions about God; we raised children even more rebellious than we were. They took

God out of everything, and now they are the ones running this nation.

The second generation, G2, now lives without God and has become worse than G3 and G4 because they chose their own god, called *self.* They became self-gods. They trust only in themselves. They rely only on themselves. They believe in themselves; self is their whole world—the context for everything.

Do you see why we need spiritual mothers?

The youngest generation, G1 (from conception to age 12), is the product of three generations of progressive distancing from God. When you take prayer and God out of the equation, what you have left is an immoral culture with no concern for true life. *I say this prophetically.* Some G1s will refuse to go to church. You won't be able to drag them; they won't want God; they won't even care to know that there is a God.

We need a shift. We need a revival that sweeps through this nation. But before that happens, you and I have to change the way we treat Jesus, and the way we worship God. We need to send the right signals to heaven. Churches that send the right signals to heaven show God that we are the true and living Church, which listens to and obeys His instructions. We honor Jesus and walk in the power of the Holy Ghost.

Jesus is listening to the Holy Ghost and interceding with the Father. He says, "That's a good church.

That's the one. They are sold out. Those missionaries are interceding all day, twenty-four-seven." Activity is always going on at the throne of God: decisions are being made. The Holy Spirit communicates with us and instructs us how to be God's ambassadors, His agents of change.

If you don't have the Holy Ghost, I don't know how you think you can hear from Jesus, because Jesus is at the right hand of the Father, and He sent the Holy Spirit to live in you. You are the temple of the Holy Spirit—not the temple of an emotion. God came down from glory, in a rushing, mighty wind and flames of fire; and He comes anew to live inside of you.

You are from God, little children, and have overcome them; because greater is He who is in you than he who is in the world. (1 John 4:4, NASB)

Greater is He that is in you than he that is in the world. The hope of the world is Christ in you. When you have the Holy Ghost, you don't yield control of your children's education to unspiritual mothers of the world like Madalyn Murray O'Hair—someone who neither accepts nor welcomes nor admits in her heart the gifts, teachings, and revelations of the Spirit of God. Instead, you stand up against these false doctrines; you resist; you fight with your life for the faith of your children and the generations to follow.

God is beginning to assemble people in apostolic centers that are set up all over America—the remnant who have decided they'll go all out. They are through playing church, sleeping through the service, playing games, and getting angry at people who offend them. The church needs to decide that it will be reformed. We need a new mindset: one that lives for God, and gives all to Him.

There is a remnant that longs for a true demonstration of the Spirit in power—not one in idle imagination. The current generation wants "the real thing." They call Coke the real thing. If you look at sports, it's apparent there, as well: airborne snowmobiles; motorcycle races; 40-mile-an-hour skydiving without a parachute. Do you think they'll be attracted to today's brand of boring Christianity—half-baked, half-committed, half-sold-out? Come on. The G1s and G2s don't play games like football, baseball, and basketball; instead, they make up their own games: the more risk the better. They jump motorcycles over helicopters and see how close they can get to the spinning blades. Do you think they'll want to come to church to sing "*Kum ba yah*"?

Ask yourself this question today: How do I present the Gospel of fire and miracles to a generation that is doing those things? Can we keep coming to church on Sunday to get warm and comfortable, and just sit there being entertained until it's time to go to dinner with our friends?

No! We have a responsibility to stop coming to church as consumers and instead become like spiritual mothers—people so dedicated to their children that they sacrifice everything for them. G2s and G1s have almost no chance of finding God, unless we stop playing church and realize we must give something wild and different to this next generation. Once the church builds G5 superstructures for their transformation, no one will be able to extract God out of their lives.

Become a springboard for the next generation. You have the Holy Spirit; you can realize and comprehend and appreciate truths the world doesn't even know. You can outmatch the world in any contest for souls, because they're limited to human wisdom. You have access to the wisdom of God!

Now we have not received the spirit [that belongs to] the world, but the [Holy] Spirit Who is from God, [given to us] that we might realize and comprehend and appreciate the gifts [of divine favor and blessing so freely and lavishly] bestowed on us by God.

And we are setting these truths forth in words not taught by human wisdom but taught by the [Holy] Spirit, combining and interpreting spiritual truths with spiritual language [to those who possess the Holy Spirit].

But the natural, nonspiritual man does not accept or welcome or admit into his heart the gifts and teachings and revelations of the Spirit of God, for they are folly (meaningless nonsense) to him; and he is incapable of knowing them [of progressively recognizing, understanding, and becoming better acquainted with them] because they are spiritually discerned and estimated and appreciated. (1 Corinthians 2:12-14, AMPC)

Right now, the church isn't setting the pace for society. The culture is setting the pace, and we're following. How we live, dress, talk, act—what we watch and do—are all guided by the world, not the church. We need to understand our leadership identity as Christians. We've been washed in the blood, born again, and Spirit-filled. Weak Christians say, "Well, maybe the Spirit-filled part is not there," or, "I don't know about the blood; I don't know if the blood is real."

Years ago, a Christian would say, "I'm blood washed, born again, saved, and redeemed." They could lay that out in seconds. Today, if you ask somebody, they say, "Well, I go to church." They can't identify who they are in absolute terms. As a result, their rope has become untied and their boat is drifting from the dock of eternity. They're floating in the sea of humanity and culture, with no idea how to find their bearings. Their compass isn't working, and they are unsure of everything.

When God brings this 5-G Shift, it will be different from any movement of the past. Principles stay the same, but we apply them to new conditions. We discover them and act upon them with relentless force. In this Shift, people will change the way they think and talk. They will change their whole existence. Only the church can about bring this 5-G Shift.

chapter 4

The Silver Cord

WHEN I WAS still a new Christian, I saw splendor and power in the great men and women of God I met. These encounters became my spiritual inheritance.

One of my Bible school teachers at Rock Church, in the early days, was an old Irishman named Dr. McKeown. Whenever Dr. McKeown taught us about revival, I saw his eyes begin to mist. Sometimes, he was overwhelmed with emotion. One day, I stayed after class and asked him, "What is it? Where do you go? What happens to you when you begin to talk about the things of God?" Dr. McKeown told me about being a little boy in the Welsh revival. That blew me away. I was talking to a first-generation witness of a mighty move of God and receiving a spiritual impartation from him through transpneumigration.

God sewed together these people with a silver cord, and we became carriers of their spiritual inheritance.

We became responsible to pass it on to the next generation. And that's exactly what we've begun to do.

Lester Sumrall once told me about the time he arrived for a meeting with Smith Wigglesworth. Lester had a newspaper under his arm when the door opened. Wigglesworth told him, "Take the newspaper and put it on the ground. You cannot come in here with that." So Dr. Sumrall threw it down and walked into the house. He noted that it was 8:05 a.m.

Lester told me, "Wigglesworth put his hands on my shoulders, and when he took his hands off, it was 12:00 p.m. I have no idea where I went or what happened, but when he took his hands off, I knew that my life had been completely changed."

Dr. Sumrall had received something from this great man of God. When he told me about this experience, I wanted to crawl across the table and hug him so I could receive what he had. I wanted to receive that spirit. David Schoch once told us about the time John G. Lake showed up at his house, and they had a communion service. God told Dr. Lake to go there two months earlier, and had even given him the address.

I've also met people who knew Tommy Hicks, a man whom God sent to Argentina. I've met people who knew Kathryn Kuhlman and Aimee Semple McPherson. Everywhere I've gone, I have seen a silver cord of redemption that God is using to pull together a fabric of people in our day who have something fresh and genuine.

I knew that God wanted to pour out something fresh on my ministry, and I began to hunger for it. Then, to my joy, it happened. After I'd been pastoring in Baltimore for about ten years, Fuchsia Pickett came to speak at a breakfast. When she stood up on our gymnasium stage and got ready to share, suddenly, about 150 men and women in the audience, who were seated at the break-fast tables, fell face-forward onto their food—just as if they'd been shot with a gun. Orange juice spilled. They had eggs on their chins.

A little nine-year-old boy, the son of one of my elders, ran up on the stage screaming, "Do you see that angel standing there?" Dr. Pickett was overwhelmed. She said, "That's the ninth time that angel has showed up in a meeting with me!" For the next 45 minutes, nobody was able to move. Then, just like that, it lifted, and we could get up again. The meeting was over. We were no good. We didn't eat. Nobody wanted to eat. God had showed up.

What Would You Do If God Showed Up?

Duncan Campbell asked people this question during the Hebrides revival in Scotland: *"What would you do if God showed up?"* On January 19, 1997, I went to my church and God showed up. When God comes to a church, it's a whole different story. When God shows up, you are never the same.

Tommy Tenney and I had been at a meeting in Brownsville, Florida, after which we got in my car and drove to Baltimore. On Saturday night, my music director, Don, called me from the Chicago airport to check in. He said, "I'm coming home." Suddenly, I heard him crying on the other end of the phone, and all this noise behind him. People were saying, "Sir, are you all right? Get the medics! Get the police!"

I heard him saying, "Thanks, I'm all right. Just leave me alone."

They were saying, "Sir, let us help you."

Then he said to me on the phone, with an incredulous tone, "Pastor, what is on you?"

I said, "I don't know, Don; but whatever it is, you're on your own. God bless you. I wish you well. I'll see you in church." I hung up on him. He later said that he'd had to reassure the people for almost an hour that he was okay. The Spirit of God had knocked him off his feet.

That Sunday, Tommy Tenney and I went into my church. Suddenly, everybody started falling on the floor, weeping and crying. Even little kids, with nobody in the room with them except the teacher, fell down on the floor and started crying so much that there were puddles of water the size of dinner plates around their heads. This outpouring continued day and night for six months; then, for three-and-a-half years. People came from all over the world. Sick people in wheelchairs were rolled in; nobody prayed for them, and they were healed.

Leonard Fox came. When I looked down, he was on the floor rolling around. Somebody said, "Pastor Fox, do you want to speak?"

He said, "I'm not worthy to speak in this environment."

One of Benny Hinn's people came and said, "We would like to address the people about Benny Hinn's upcoming meeting in Baltimore."

Tommy said, "Okay. Go ahead."

The guy got up on the stage and said, "I'd like to . . .I'd like to . . ." and down he went, right onto the floor.

I called Violet Kiteley and said, "Something has broken out at my church. Please come." She jumped on a plane and came right away. She went into our meeting, and after she'd been there for an hour, she came to the back and said, "This is exactly what we had in the Latter Rain. It is the same spirit, the same presence we had in 1948."

I didn't know what had happened; I didn't know how to handle it. I'd wanted to create a hunger for God in people like in the book of Acts, and it was happening.

Now when they heard this, they were pierced to the heart, and said to Peter and the rest of the apostles, "Brethren, what shall we do?"

Peter said to them, "Repent, and each of you be baptized in the name of Jesus Christ for the forgiveness of your sins; and you will receive the gift of the Holy Spirit. For the promise is for you and your children and for all who are far off, as many as the Lord our God will call to Himself." (Acts 2:37-39, NASB)

Peter told his hearers that the promise of the Holy Spirit wasn't only for them, but also for their children, and all who were afar off—including the Gentiles. It was for as many as the Lord God called to Himself. The gift of the Holy Spirit wasn't only for those who were present at that moment; He was a gift to be transferred to others afar off, for generations to come.

God's outpouring in Acts 2 was an experience for those alive at that time; it was also for them to pass on to the next generation, and the next. God didn't expect this spiritual outpouring to remain with one generation. He expected them to transfer it to others through the supernatural process of transpneumigration. This process included writing it down—a collection of letters that became the New Testament—but it went beyond even that. The apostles personally laid hands on the next generation and imparted something spiritual into their lives.

In the city of Baltimore, we have 1,300 churches. If 70 percent of these churches shut their doors tomorrow, nobody would even know it. Most cities are the same. Churches are not giving anything significant to the next generation. They're focused on themselves. If younger generations are to be reached, we must invest in them with our time, money, and love. We must ask God to give us a burden for our city, for its souls—for the lost. How can we watch them perish and have no feeling?

Churches ask people, "Would you serve?" and get the response, "I don't have time." Why? Because we're out of love with our First Love. We don't love people as we love ourselves, in the way He told us to love them. Big cities with churches on every corner usually have hell on every corner, too—right beside the church. Next door to many of the fastest growing churches in America—massive megachurches—the crime rates are some of the highest in the country. If you have that many people going to church on Sunday, shouldn't they be coming out fired up and full of God, doing something to change the community?

The Church Has Been Pushing Out God's Prophetic Warriors
Something vital is missing from the church today. That's why communities aren't being changed. That

missing thing relates to the title of this chapter: "The Silver Cord." It's the prophetic voice of men and women who are fully yielded to God. That voice is almost entirely missing from the church today. Why? Because most churches drive out prophetic warriors. They avoid conflict. They compromise. They don't want to be criticized for publicly resisting evil.

It will take the restoration of the prophets to complete the restoration of the sons and daughters of God. Associating with anointed men and women of God has a positive impact on us and the generations around us. As long as the church is passive, bound, ineffectual, and selfish, the enemy wins.

The generations in the church today, and in the recent past, have been led by passive, milquetoast, compromising individuals who want to please everybody. They take the heart out of the Gospel and tone it down, making it of no effect. The largest segment of people who attend today's churches belong to generations G4 and G3. They just want to finish their time, complete the process, and get their ticket punched so they can go to glory.

God left us examples in the Bible who were not like that at all. Jehu (2 Kings 9 and 10) was a prophetic warrior sent by God. We still have some prophetic warriors like Jehu left in the body of Christ. I have mentioned some of them. We drive today's Jehus away from the church so they won't pull us into a conflict. We need to stop pushing prophetic warriors out of the church with our stiff-necked resistance and hard-heartedness.

The Jezebel Spirit of Diabolic Deception

In Chapter 2, we considered the vital importance of spiritual fathers and the impartation that's transferred generationally from fathers to sons and daughters. We saw how the Rechabites respected their ancestor, Jehonadab, and how their commitment to his covenant affected their future and even impressed God. They were different because they honored the example of their father.

Where did Jehonadab receive the spirit that made him a man of such strong convictions—a man whose impact lasted for generations? It was related to his experience with Jehu, God's prophetic warrior. Jehu called Jehonadab up into his chariot and said, "Come with me, and see my zeal for the Lord" (2 Kings 10:16, KJV). Jehonadab saw for himself the judgment of God upon witchcraft, immorality, and the abuse of authority. He was never the same after that.

In Chapter 3, we saw the effect of godly mothers on their families and those around them. We saw the impact of ungodly mothers, like Madalyn Murray O'Hair, with her demonic zeal to drive God, prayer, and the Bible from the public arena in America. In the Old Testament, Jezebel almost destroyed the spiritual heritage of Israel by her evil influence on the household of King Ahab, her husband. This woman, Jezebel, and her diabolic deceptions almost single-handedly brought Israel down. She did succeed in bringing the judgment of God on Israel. The same evil powers are working today to wound, delay, and kill emerging leadership in God's house.

Jehu and Jehonadab

Once again, the Bible tells us that the sons of Jehonadab, the Rechabites, were offered wine, but they refused.

But they said, We will drink no wine: for Jonadab the son of Rechab our father commanded us, saying, Ye shall drink no wine, neither ye, nor your sons for ever: Neither shall ye build house, nor sow seed, nor plant vineyard, nor have any: but all your days ye shall dwell in tents; that ye may live many days in the land where ye be strangers. Thus have we obeyed the voice of Jonadab the son of Rechab our father in all that he hath charged us, to drink no wine all our days, we, our wives, our sons, nor our daughters; Nor to build houses for us to dwell in: neither have we vineyard, nor field, nor seed. (Jeremiah 35:6-9, KJV)

That shook things up, because everybody drank wine. But these boys said, "No, we won't drink." They were under a covenant. They refused because their father Jehonadab had instructed them, and this was a vow before God. It's very similar to a Nazarite vow, such as the one Samson took.

Most vows usually lasted for a short period of time, but this vow didn't. It lasted for generations. Remember, they said that all their generations had been doing this. Something had happened to Jehonadab that blew their minds. Something impacted them in such a way that they said, "Hold on. This is different. We're under a covenant." God was impressed with what these men and women did.

And Jeremiah said unto the house of the Rechabites, Thus saith the LORD of hosts, the God of Israel; Because ye have obeyed the commandment of Jonadab your father, and kept all his precepts, and done according unto all that he hath commanded you: Therefore thus saith the LORD of hosts, the God of Israel; Jonadab the son of Rechab shall not want a man to stand before me for ever. (Jeremiah 35:18-19, KJV)

In other words, God said, "I'm going to have part of your genealogy. Your families are going to be in the church all the days of their lives. You're going to find that your children's children will come up under the covenant of God, and they will serve the Lord. I am pleased with what you did."

It was because this encounter showed their adherence to a covenant that God would even make this promise.

He gave His generational blessing to godly men and women who were passing down generationally what God had done. God asked, if the sons of Jehonadab would keep their father's commands, why wouldn't the nation of Israel keep its heavenly Father's commands? He used the obedience of the Rechabites as an object lesson to set in motion His judgment upon the disobedience of Israel.

God used their obedience the same way He'll use the obedience of the church as the key to bring judgment upon unbelievers in America. In 2 Corinthians 10:6 (NASB), it says, "we are ready to punish all disobedience, whenever your obedience is complete." Remember, God promised blessing to the descendants of Jehonadab because they were faithful to the words left to them. If we don't leave instructions from God for the next generation, when they turn eighteen, they'll leave the church. We haven't brought our kids under a covenant so that they feel the impact of covenant obedience. That's why they run away.

Jehonadab's lineage kept their father's words long after he died. The father didn't tell the sons to avoid sin; he gave them instructions to abstain from what were normal and wholesome activities. Telling your kids not to sin is not as powerful as telling them to do away with what seems good for them. Today, this would be like telling your kids not to buy a car, and they should never drink Coke. Abstaining from something good takes sacrifice. Abstaining from something sin is easy.

The background of Jehonadab is found in 2 Kings 9 and 10. God becomes angry with Jehoram (also called Joram), king of Israel, son of Ahab, and the wicked Queen Jezebel. God's prophet goes and anoints the warrior Jehu to kill Jehoram:

> *He arose and went into the house, and he poured the oil on his head and said to him, "Thus says the LORD, the God of Israel, 'I have anointed you king over the people of the LORD even over Israel. You shall strike the house of Ahab your master, that I may avenge the blood of My servants the prophets, and the blood of all the servants of the LORD, at the hand of Jezebel. For the whole house of Ahab shall perish, and I will cut off from Ahab every male person both bond and free in Israel. I will make the house of Ahab like the house of Jeroboam the son of Nebat, and like the house of Baasha the son of Ahijah. The dogs shall eat Jezebel in the territory of Jezreel, and none shall bury her.'" Then he opened the door and fled. (2 Kings 9:6-10, NASB)*

Jehu was a warrior with a chariot and an attitude. He was a bad dude. God sent Jehu to destroy the house of Ahab, so he rode out in his chariot to fulfill God's mission. Jehu killed Jehoram, king of Israel, and then

Ahaziah, king of Judah—another member of the family of Ahab. God specifically sent Jehu after the wicked Jezebel, who'd tried to kill the prophet Elijah after he exposed the prophets of Baal (1 Kings 18)—men who'd done many other evil deeds.

> *When Jehu came to Jezreel, Jezebel heard of it, and she painted her eyes and adorned her head and looked out the window. As Jehu entered the gate, she said, "Is it well, Zimri, your master's murderer?" Then he lifted up his face to the window and said, "Who is on my side? Who?" And two or three officials looked down at him.*
>
> *He said, "Throw her down." So they threw her down, and some of her blood was sprinkled on the wall and on the horses, and he trampled her under foot."* (2 Kings 9:30-32-33, NASB)

This is where we pick up with the story of Jehonadab, the righteous ancestor of the men Jeremiah encountered, who were faithful to the vow of their father not to drink wine.

> *Now when [Jehu] had departed from there, he met Jehonadab the son of Rechab coming to meet him; and he greeted him and said to him, "Is your heart right, as my heart is with your heart?" And Jehonadab answered, "It is." Jehu said, "If it is, give*

me your hand." And he gave him his hand, and he took him up to him into the chariot.

[Jehu said to Jehonadab], "Come with me and see my zeal for the LORD." So he made him ride in his chariot. When he came to Samaria, he killed all who remained to Ahab in Samaria, until he had destroyed him, according to the word of the LORD which He spoke to Elijah. (2 Kings 10:15-17, NASB)

Jehu is riding in his chariot, with blood all over him and all over his horses. His weapons are stacked inside. As he's riding, he sees this boy Jehonadab, the father of the boys who wouldn't drink wine with Jeremiah. Jehu brings his horses to a stop and says, "Come on! Come up here with me." Jehonadab is invited to get into the chariot of a killing machine. When Jehu invites Jehonadab to ride in the chariot, he asks him, "Is your heart right?"

You don't want to get on my chariot if your heart is not committed to the Lordship of Jesus, to the Kingdom of God and the advancement of the Gospel. You don't want to get on my chariot, because I'm going after witchcraft. I'm going after demonic figures. I'm going to destroy the enemies of the Church of the Lord Jesus Christ, and if you want to get on my chariot, you better realize we are going to war. We're not going to raise up snowflakes; we're going to raise up those who know how to tear down principalities, powers, and wickedness in high places.

Jehu says, "Get on board, boy, and I'm going to give you a show." Then the Bible says that Jehu "killed all who remained to Ahab in Samaria, until he had destroyed him." Jehonadab rides in Jehu's chariot. Jehu's anointing to fulfill the prophetic word affects Jehonadab. He's pulled into the conflict. He rides into battle and somehow receives an impartation of Jehu's courage and power. In the midst of the battle, Jehonadab's life is changed, and he tells his boys, "I've been somewhere. I'm different."

This decision is also yours: the choice to make a covenant to serve God with all your heart—the decision to tear down everything that is anti-church and against God's movement. Those things are what we are all about. Jehu says, "Son, get in my chariot and I'm going to teach you how to tear down the strongholds of religion and principalities and powers. Get in my chariot today." Jehu says, "I'll take you to the land where we will be victorious." And those boys become a product of his experience. They teach their children's children the same thing. Generationally, it affects all of Israel.

What has the church done today? We've got nobody in the chariot because we're not listening for the assignment. When Jehonadab saw for himself the judgment of God upon witchcraft, immorality, and the abuse of authority, he was never the same. Jesus is our Jehu. It is time for fathers and mothers to pull the sons of God's house up into our chariots, to ride with us while we defeat the enemies of God's Kingdom.

Today, we have another natural example. Everybody is freaking out: "Oh my God, Donald Trump is president, and he is going to draw us into war!" Well, I can tell you one thing: If we go to war, I have very strong confidence that we will kick butt, take names, and win. Am I for it? No. Do I want it? No. Am I advocating it? No. But I'll tell you what: Satan has got a Jehu on his hands, and he doesn't know what to do with it. He's got a Jehu on his hands with an assignment, who's pulled up his chariot and said, "Boys, get in, because we're going to do this thing."

I said earlier that, when we came in as hippies and got saved in Rock Church, Brother John had to warn people about what they'd see. We didn't know until later that he said to every guest preacher, "We have some people in the front rows who might shock you. Some of them have been in jail. These are hardcore, tough guys, and if you're not anointed, they get really upset."

That was intimidating; but what they also found out, if they stayed around long enough, was that we were warriors. We were committed to go to war. One time, at a service, Brother John said, "How many of you will give a thousand dollars to build the school?" In the front rows, a lot of hands shot up right away. One of the elders said,

"I rebuke that. Number one, that's dirty money because it's drug money; and number two, they ain't got that money. Look how they dress."

Well, it turned out that some of us, before the day was over, gave Brother John the money. He went back to them and said, "Hey, I want to tell you something. Y'all need to move into the 10th row back there, because these are the saints. They are giving." We didn't have a lot of money, but we gave everything we had. We gave it because it was time to give a pledge and we were going to be part of it. We had joined a gang. We didn't know it was called a church. We just joined.

I talk to pastors who say, "Oh my God, my kids are leaving the church." Why do they leave? Because you run them out; you don't put up a welcome sign. I want to say to the G4 and G3 generations that the G2s are waiting for you. Stop your chariot, reach out your hand, and bring them up to go to war with you. Instead, you are running. Some of you have your chariots, but you are not running *toward* the enemy. You are running *from* the enemy.

Stop your chariot, pull up those horses, and say, "Come on, get on with me."

They'll ask you, "Where are you going?"

You'll say, "We're going to win. We're going to bring the church back into the forefront. We're going to bring the church back into the culture. We're going to let the culture know that the Church of Jesus Christ is still alive and miracles still happen today. Hell is as real as it's ever been, and heaven is as good as it will ever get. God is alive, and He wants to do something to change the way we think."

If you ask the youth who are still left in the church, they'll tell you, "I don't want a babysitter. I want somebody who can give me the fire. I want somebody to give me the anointing. I want somebody who lives what they talk about." Those are our young people. Those are your G2s.

Father, I pray right now over the G4's and G3's. I don't know what it will take, God, but may I not die before I see them awakened out of their sleeping slumber, of being at ease in Zion. I ask, God, today, that you would cause a Holy Spirit encounter so that careers and ambitions of ungodly behavior will drop to the side and they will begin to pray this prayer:

"God, with my remaining years I will serve the living God, Jehovah. May He be everything to me. May I be like Jehu and may my chariot be one of war so that we win a great victory. May my chariot be that anointed thing that You will do with me and through me, and I will reach out.

"I repent of my sin. I repent of my apathy and lethargy. I repent of my laziness. I repent of my selfishness and I say today, God, here is my life. Use me to influence another generation. May it not be empty rhetoric. May it be reality. I sow with my mouth today a seed of commitment. In Jesus' name, amen."

In your city, get ready to serve notice to Satan and his lying thieves that he cannot have your young men and young women. Satan is operating off limits, and he is illegal. He cannot touch them. He cannot come near your dwelling. He cannot come near your house. He cannot come into the habitation of the house of God. He cannot snatch them out. He cannot root them out. He cannot pull them out.

If there is an ounce of God in you, release it to do His work today. If there is an ounce of prayer, let it out today. If there's an ounce of commitment, let it out! Let a cry arise. God's Jehus, get ready. Take up the G2 and G1 generations into your chariots. Take up the sons and daughters of the house of God. Let the brightness of the light of God in your life draw the Gentile and the sinner into the Kingdom.

Father, we declare that the brightness of your Shekinah glory will cover the tent of your churches. It will be resident there so that when people ride by, they will see the brightness of the glory of God. When people walk in the door, they will see the brightness of the glory of God. Dads will bring their sons and moms will bring their daughters. And orphaned daughters and sons will come without parents and the people of the church will ride their chariots over and reach out to them.

Like Jehu, ask the young people, "Is your heart right?" Then, reach out your hand like Jehu, and say to that young one, "Come on! Get up inside the chariot of God's grace in my life. I give you my hand."

Chapter 5

The 5-G Shift

The biggest shift in history happened 2,000 years ago when Jesus Christ died on the cross for our sins and rose from the dead so that whosoever believes in Him should not perish but have everlasting life. All of human history is dated from that shift.

One of the biggest lies today—besides believing that Jesus' death was not enough and we need to earn our own salvation by our money or our works—is believing that the church is a physical building where people go to sit once a week for entertainment, with their tickets punched for heaven, and make no investment in the generations behind them.

We need a new reformation and a 5-G Shift to restore what has been lost.

*I*N APRIL *1521,* in Worms, Germany, a 37-year-old monk named Martin Luther arrived to face a public inquiry. Angry officials of the Roman Catholic Church and Charles V, Emperor of the Holy Roman Empire, had demanded that he recant his teaching that faith in Jesus Christ was the only way to be saved. Masses of people were there to greet him. They were not angry—they were ecstatic! They gave Martin Luther a hero's welcome. Luther had delivered them from bondage to the church's false teachings and released them to faith in Jesus Christ. A historian wrote,

> *A surging mass of people gathered and pressed about the wagon. In boundless joy men and women, old and young cheered him, and blessed the day on which they had been permitted to see the man who had dared to break the fetters of the Pope, and to deliver poor Christianity from his bondage. On stepping from his wagon at his lodging place Luther said, 'God will be with me!'*[5]

Sola Fide—Faith Alone

Luther had discovered the truth of the Bible after years of desperate soul-searching and study. He passionately sought to please God, and found the answers in Romans and Galatians—especially this passage from Romans 1:17:

---

5. Gustav Just, *Life of Luther*. Translated from the German by S. and H. St. Louis, Mo.: Concordia Publishing House, 1903. Online at *http://www.gutenberg.org/files/38544/38544-h/38544-h.htm*. Accessed May 2019.

For therein is the righteousness of God revealed from faith to faith: as it is written, the just shall live by faith. (Romans 1:17, KJV)

The answer to pleasing God was faith alone! This turned the world upside down.

Wouldn't you like to have an encounter with God that turned your world upside down? Most of us today want only enough of God to make us happy when we need to be happy, but we don't want God to interrupt our plans or schedule. We pray, "Listen, God, I'm doing this and that, and I have this and that agenda, so don't disrupt me!" We've lost our fear of the Lord!

Luther was the opposite. He desperately wanted God to accept him. He knew he was a sinner; so what a thrill when he discovered that faith in Jesus was the way the Father had provided for sinners like him to become acceptable! He'd tried and failed many times to save himself through repentance. He'd performed every penance assigned by the priest. Then, he discovered the truth. Jesus had already paid the price for his sins and satisfied God's standards of righteousness. Jesus had died in his place so that he could live!

Once the people of Germany learned what Luther had discovered, they knew it was right. That's why they cheered and spread the word far and wide. What do you think would happen if today's masses of mixed-up people discovered the same faith that energized Luther and those Germans? Wouldn't mobs of cheering people march again in the streets for the sake of something worth cheering about? Of course they would!

Sola Gratia—Grace Alone

Another of the great biblical truths rediscovered by Luther and other great Christian leaders of the Protestant Reformation was the message of grace— God's unmerited favor. Grace comes only as a gift. You can't work for it. God *imputes* grace to you in a supernatural transfer. All you can do is make yourself available to receive this gift God wants to give you. Only God can release you from spiritual death to spiritual life.

> *For by grace you have been saved through faith; and that not of yourselves, it is the gift of God; not as a result of works, so that no one may boast. (Ephesians 2:8-9, NASB)*

Sola Scriptura—The Word of God Alone

When Luther entered the "Diet," or public meeting, at Worms, 5,000 people were there. Officials from the emperor and the church told Luther to recant his teaching that we are saved by faith in Jesus Christ— not by faith plus works decreed by the church. Luther refused to do so unless they could prove to him from the Bible that he was wrong. He knew that the Bible alone was the source of truth, not the Bible plus the words of the pope.

The words Luther spoke that day still ring through the centuries:

Unless I am convinced by the testimony of the Holy Scriptures, or by patent, clear, and cogent reasons and arguments (for I believe neither the Pope nor the councils alone, since it is evident that they have often erred and contradicted themselves), and because the passages adduced and quoted by me have convinced and bound my conscience in God's Word, therefore I cannot and will not recant, since it is neither safe nor advisable to do anything against conscience. **Here I stand; I cannot do otherwise! God help me! Amen."** *(1521)*[6]

As a result of his bold stand, Luther was considered a heretic. He had already been excommunicated by the pope of the Roman Catholic Church. The Edict of Worms labeled him a "poisonous pest" and called for him to be captured. People were forbidden to hide or protect him. His books were to be burned. The emperor gave him 21 days of safe travel following the Diet of Worms. After that, he was on his own. Soon after Luther started on his journey, he was captured.

---

6. Gustav Just, *Life of Luther.*

After a little while the wagon turned into a narrow pass. Suddenly armed horsemen dashed out of the forest, fell upon the wagon, and amid curses and threats commanded the driver to halt, and tore Luther from his seat. Without molesting the others they threw a mantle upon Luther, placed him upon a horse, and led him in zigzag through the forest. It was nearly midnight when the drawbridge of the Wartburg fell and the castle received the weary horsemen within its protecting walls.[7]

Luther was captured! But not by his enemies. This was actually a staged rescue by Frederick III, also known as Frederick the Wise, who was elector (leader) of the German state of Saxony and founder of the University of Wittenberg. This capture was invented to confuse Luther's enemies so that Frederick III could hide him at Wartburg Castle.

Within the first 11 weeks of Luther's ten-month exile there, he'd translated the entire New Testament into German! It was an incredible, supernatural feat. Although this wasn't the first German translation, it was a literary masterpiece that popularized the Bible everywhere. Now, people could have Bibles in their hands and no longer rely on the local priest to tell them what it said. They could read the Word, pray, and work things

---

7. Gustav Just, *Life of Luther.*

out with God on their own, by faith. We take the Bible for granted today, but it cost something.

The world is changing so quickly that many people awaken with anxiety each new day. How can we find stability in the midst of change around us? Only the Lord and His wisdom can stabilize us, now and forever, and strengthen us in the fear of the Lord.

Wisdom and knowledge shall be the stability of thy times, and strength of salvation; the fear of the Lord is his treasure. (Isaiah 33:6, KJV)

Stability means "firmness of position; resistance to disintegration; not likely to fall; firm or steady." Not even earth-shattering change can weaken you. You are strong. God says in Daniel 11:32, "But the people who know their God shall be strong, and carry out great exploits."

As a young man, Luther had become a monk after an encounter with God. In 1505, he'd been riding a horse when lightning struck nearby, knocking him to the ground. *Boom!* He said later that it was a confrontation with death and divine judgment. He had an epiphany that God was Who He said He was. Luther cried out, vowing to become a monk! Before that day, he'd been on a career path chosen by his father to become a lawyer; but that bolt of lightning set him on a completely different course that would have an impact for generations.

Luther entered St. Augustine's Ministry in Erfurt, and was consecrated into the Roman Catholic priesthood in 1507. From there, he was called to teach theology at the University of Wittenberg, founded by Frederick the Wise, who later rescued him. Luther earned his masters and doctorate degrees and took a vow that he kept for the rest of his life—"I swear to defend the gospel truth with all my might."

Luther's first bold public stand for the Bible happened on October 31, 1517, when he was 33 years old—three and a half years before the Diet of Worms. He was a professor of theology at the University of Wittenberg. Luther wrote Ninety-five Theses—points of challenge against the church's positions. These theses, or paragraphs, were based on the Bible, and had been spawned in his private prayer time with God. Luther took his paper with the Ninety-five Theses to the main door of the University's Chapel Church, a location that served as a bulletin board among those at the university. He nailed it to the door, and the world has never been the same.

When he took those stands, Luther was in what I call the G3 generation. As a teacher, and later as a pastor, he had a daily opportunity for impartation into the G2 generation behind him. He could transfer his spirit to them. They would not have to endure the same desolations he had experienced. He could help them build their lives on a foundation of faith in Jesus Christ and the Word of God.

Then they will rebuild the ancient ruins, They will raise up the former devastations; And they will repair the ruined cities, The desolations of many generations. (Isaiah 61:4, NASB)

The Bible is filled with words of restoration and hope that G2 and G1 need today. From one generation to another, we can help people to rebuild their lives on hope. Jeremiah spoke of God's plans for our hope:

"For I know the plans that I have for you," declares the LORD, "plans for welfare and not for calamity to give you a future and a hope. Then you will call upon Me and come and pray to Me, and I will listen to you. You will seek Me and find Me when you search for Me with all your heart." (Jeremiah 29:11-13, NASB)

God says, "Come and pray to Me, and I will listen to you." We want to have God listening. Then He says, "You will seek Me and find Me when you search for Me with your whole heart." A lot of people are not hearing God because they are halfhearted and double-minded. They want some of God and some of something else. They're divided. The Bible says that someone like that is unstable in all of his ways (James 1:8). John wrote of God's plans for our prosperity:

"Beloved, I pray that in all respects you may prosper and be in good health, just as your soul prospers." (3 John 2, NASB)

Hope and spiritual prosperity came when Luther stirred things up—when faith in Jesus Christ became a reality to the people. His persecution and suffering hadn't ended, but a period of global influence of the true church had been released. The Reformers went on to build nations on the foundation of the Bible, including the United States.

They called Luther a crazy man. They called him a lunatic. They said that he was out of his mind to believe such things; but I want to tell you something. God prevailed on his behalf. He didn't just shake a neighborhood. He didn't just shake a city. He shook nations. He shook the known world. Unless you learn these stories from church history, you won't know the roots of your Christianity, and you won't know the power of faith and hope. You won't know where you came from and where you can go as you take other people forward in Christ.

The Bible says we learn history to teach it to coming generations.

"One generation shall praise Your works to another, And shall declare Your mighty acts." (Psalm 145:4, NASB)

My cry, after 45 years in ministry, is that God would raise up young men and women who take up their cross and leave worldly things on the other side of the Jordan, then go over with God. My cry is that these individuals would live for God in missions and in ministry, and bring a new reformation.

Before we can have a revival, we must have a new reformation. We need to reform our thinking. Luther changed the way he thought when he discovered what the Bible said. He now had a kingdom perspective of God and of the world. Most people sitting in church have no sense at all about a Christian kingdom worldview. They use Christianity to get out of their mistakes and solve all of their problems. If we're going to see revival sweep through nations again, as prophets have prophesied, we will need a new reformation—a big shift. In that reformation, we will have to change the way we treat Jesus. We will have to rediscover the gift of faith.

Luther wrote of the transforming power he received from the revelation that his righteousness was a gift from God received by faith in Jesus Christ. He described the feeling:

At last, meditating day and night and by the mercy of God, I . . . began to understand that the righteousness of God is that through which the righteous live by a gift of God, namely by faith. . . . Here I felt as if I were entirely born again and had entered paradise itself through gates that had been flung open.[8]

Are we giving the next generation the hope and power that come from being open to receive faith? Have we forgotten the exhilaration of being born again? One of the powerful effects of Luther's encounter with God was his gift with words. He translated the Bible into German with words that stirred men's hearts. He wrote hymns that revealed God's awesome power on the earth, such as "A Mighty Fortress Is Our God."

A mighty fortress is our God, a bulwark never failing;

Our helper He, amid the flood of mortal ills prevailing:

For still our ancient foe doth seek to work us woe;

His craft and pow'r are great, and, armed with cruel hate,

On earth is not his equal.

And though this world, with devils filled, should threaten to undo us,

---

8. Quoted in Dr. James M. Kittelson, "The Breakthrough. When, where, and how did Luther make his astounding discovery of justification by faith?" *Christian History* Issue 34: Martin Luther: The Reformer's Early Years. Excerpt from Luther's Preface to his collected Latin works, written the year before he died.

We will not fear, for God hath willed His truth to triumph through us;

The Prince of Darkness grim, we tremble not for him;

His rage we can endure, for lo, his doom is sure,

One little word shall fell him.

That word above all earthly pow'rs, no thanks to them, abideth;

The Spirit and the gifts are ours through Him Who with us sideth;

Let goods and kindred go, this mortal life also;

The body they may kill: God's truth abideth still,

His kingdom is forever.

As men and women on the hill of Calvary, every generation of Christians needs to examine its belief practices under the microscope of Scripture. We need to identify and purge the worldly assertions that so easily beset us, and jealously protect the freedoms so dearly acquired for us. We need to ask ourselves, "Where am I? What is my purpose in life? Am I just playing church or is something supernatural working in my life?"

When Jesus said, "Take up your cross," He was talking about sacrifice. It is a great sacrifice to live for others when you would rather live for yourself. The 5-G Shift is a sacrifice by the G5, G4, and G3 generations to empower G2 and G1.

It will be a sacrifice to reach back to the G2 generation; but look at their awful condition. The G2 generation has no identity. They don't know who they are. When you have no identity, you don't take responsibility. When you have no identity, you don't preserve life. It's easy to kill something that's not identified. That's why they abort their children. They say, "They aren't really children." They kill them because they have no identity as people themselves. The G2 generation kills other G2s for sport, because the others are not humans to them.

David Kiteley from Shiloh Christian Fellowship came to Rock City Church. He shared that, in Oakland, California, only four percent of the people go to church. That's all. That means 9 out of 10 people in Oakland may not know Jesus died for them. That is his burden. Too many of God's people have no burden. They have become insensitive. The world has indoctrinated us, possessed us, and filled us with itself. It has seduced us to abandon Jesus' call to carry our cross. Carrying your cross means walking like Christ and living for Him every day. It means dying to self. In fact, your greatest battle is the battle of self. We need to give up our selfish lives to live for Christ in humility, brokenness, commitment to others.

We must shift our focus back to the cross, and train the generations behind us to carry their crosses. We must impart a new spirit to them through transpneumigration. Jesus, on the way to the cross, had a burden for Jerusalem. He wept, because He knew God's judgment was coming. He wept with compassion for the lost.

When [Jesus] approached Jerusalem, He saw the city and wept over it, saying, "If you had known in this day, even you, the things which make for peace! But now they have been hidden from your eyes. For the days will come upon you when your enemies will throw up a barricade against you, and surround you and hem you in on every side, and they will level you to the ground and your children within you, and they will not leave in you one stone upon another, because you did not recognize the time of your visitation." (Luke 19:41-44, NASB)

Before Jesus came, Jeremiah had a burden for Jerusalem. He saw the rampant sin and wept for the city. Prostitutes were on the streets around the temple. Young people had given themselves to homosexuality and all kinds of illicit sex. He knew God's judgment was justified; yet he, too, wept with compassion.

My eyes fail because of tears,

My spirit is greatly troubled;

My heart is poured out on the earth,

Because of the destruction of the daughter of my people,

When little ones and infants faint,

In the streets of the city. (Lamentations 2:11, NASB)

Jeremiah cried out for others to share his burden for the city. He was absolutely overwhelmed.

Arise, cry aloud in the night,

At the beginning of the night watches;

Pour out your heart like water,

Before the presence of the Lord;

Lift up your hands to Him,

For the life of your little ones,

Who are faint because of hunger,

At the head of every street. (Lamentations 2:19, NASB)

Jeremiah did not hide inside a building. He went to the streets. He went out among these people in every way possible. He didn't stay away. He saw their desperation, stood with them at the threshold of God's judgment, and cried out to God from a place of humility and brokenness. In his weakness, Jeremiah made room for God to release His strength in order to accomplish His plan.

God the Father brings us to a revelation of hope—a place where the cross is real and we receive Jesus. But here's the thing: If we don't walk with Him and take up our cross, our religion is weak and false. God is looking for people today who seek Him first and seek His kingdom, so that He can add everything else to them (Matthew 6:33). Be alert, or you will miss the moment.

We know from 1 Corinthians 15:6 that, after Jesus' resurrection He appeared to more than 500 people. However, by the time the Holy Ghost finally came, only 120 were present for the outpouring of God. I wouldn't have wanted to be one of the other 380, in some alleyway of Jerusalem, who heard one of the faithful 120 testify to what had happened:

"Fire fell down! The wind blew! 120 people received other languages and we were filled with the Holy Spirit! But... where were you?"

"Oh, I got weary in waiting. I checked out. I got busy. I had something else to do."

Jesus is at the right hand of the Father. The Holy Spirit is here with us and has come to live in us. We are the temple of the Holy Spirit. We are the temple of the Third Person of God, Who came down from glory in a rushing mighty wind and flames of fire. We'd better get ahold of this, Saints. There is no day like this one that has ever been. It's too dangerous to play games with your own soul and the souls of our youth. The Scriptures tell us that people will someday say to Jesus, "You know, we did this and that in Your name." But Jesus will say, "Depart from Me, I don't even know you" (Matthew 7:22-23).

You can put on all the religious trappings. You can put on all the robes. You can put on all the gear you want. It's not going to usher you into the things of God. The church needs a shift—a 5-G generational shift. We have moved off the foundations of the Bible, His cross, our cross, and our desperate prayer for cities to be saved and spared from God's judgment. We are confused and divided.

I once participated in a video conference with several Christian leaders. We were all in little cubes on the screen, and everybody was talking. I listened to some of the things these guys were talking about. These are my peers. These are guys I've grown up with; but as I was listening to them, I was hearing the same things repeated over and over. We need something fresh. We need a new reformation and a 5-G generational shift.

Look behind you. Your future is behind you.

We need to ask God to change us from Takers to Givers. Today's ministries have only marginally raised up a generation with a greater dimension than they have. If we're going to see the next generation reached, we must invest in them our time, our money, and our love.

It's time to take the kids out of that back room in the church where we put them and expect them to stay until they turn 18, hoping they survive that long. It's time to bring G2s into the House of God and empower them so God can raise up a new generation of saints. Most of them have no concept at all that there's a biblical foundation for everything. It should be a desirable thing for G2s to be saved, holy, pure, and not have sex before marriage. They can be wealthy, be blessed, and move forward in life if they follow the principle that God makes you prosperous to advance His kingdom.

We need to bring back righteousness and judgment to Christianity in the United States. We need to bring back the basic principles of God's Word into the bylaws of the structure of God's house. God still has an assignment for my generation, the Baby Boomers. I don't want to die before I see the younger generations come running back into the house of God. That means my generation will have to turn and look behind us in order to see the future.

If we want the church to survive, we have to restore our faith and our passion for God, and for spiritual parenting. We have to make a 5-G Shift and do whatever God tells us for those younger generations. We need a new 5-G Church model to bring them in.

Let's talk next about how that 5-G Church might look.

chapter 6

Restoring the G2 Generation

*T*HE CURRENT *G2* generation is poised to inherit the financial riches of the world as it emerges from the Babylonian culture of our time into Christ-likeness. This has happened before in history: You discover that you are no longer a slave to the culture. You find your destiny in the church. You stop thinking, talking and acting as if you're still in slavery. You find your freedom, and you go after others to share that freedom in Christ.

"Hey, Bart, do you want to go to jail?"

I said, "Oh, no. No, man."

He said, "I mean, do you want to go there and speak?"

"What do you mean go and speak?"

He said, "No, we wouldn't put you in jail. You would be going there to testify."

I said, "What does 'testify' mean? I don't know what you're talking about." I knew people who testified about me and sent me to jail; but this man was obviously talking about something else! He was an old guy at Rock Church, where I'd just been saved. I think he drove a UPS truck. He had no rapport, but he had the love of God. So I said, "Okay."

I went with him to jail. I was scared to death, because I thought they were going to find another warrant or something and lock me up—and this time, I wouldn't be coming out. I prayed, "Jesus!" constantly. We were in there, and I was as nervous as a cat.

This old guy says to the men who came to the meeting, "I have a young man with me who is going to share with you." I'm thinking, *What does that mean? "Share"? I don't know what it means to share.* The man walked by me, and I asked him, "What does that mean?"

He says, "Just tell them what happened."

Then while I was looking, I saw another man among the prisoners that I knew. I thought to myself, *Don't look at him!*

I began to talk to the guys in the jail. It was my first time testifying, or "sharing," as they called it. I said bluntly, "I was going to hell, and instead, I went to a church and I said a prayer like this: 'Jesus, come in my life. If you're not real, get the hell outta here.' And this has changed my life. That's it."

This big black guy with muscular arms and a tattoo asked me, "Do you think God could do that for me?"

I said, "I don't know if He wants to or not." That wasn't the right thing to say, but I said, "I can tell you this: if you just pray this prayer you will find out. Say, 'Jesus, if you're real, come into my life.'"

About ten guys stood up and prayed that prayer. I think they all got saved. I went away and said, "Whoa, that was cool, man!" I mean, I felt things happening in the spirit world, and I didn't even know the Holy Spirit very well at the time.

The next week, I asked my new friend, the UPS truck driver, "Can I go with you again?" I got caught up in it. I understood something new about this life in Christ, and I appreciated the people God had sent to help me to grow up.

Helping People Grow Up

I once watched a Ravens NFL game in which an older football player was interviewed about his role in helping young Ravens players transition into pro sports. He said that, when he was coming up, he didn't have a mentor to help him adjust. Therefore, he'd made up his mind to help the next generation.

When you're at the age level of G2, which is 12 to 25 years old, there are things you don't know yet about life, but you're still enthusiastic enough to try anything. I believe that, if the church turns our hearts towards the G2s, they can be the greatest generation that's ever been seen on the earth. G1s are children who see their older G2 brothers and sisters and say, "Wow! I want to be just like them!" When the G2s turn toward the G1s, that just may be the spark that lights a fire in both of them to bring a spiritual revival.

As I've been saying, if we make the transition to the 5-G Local Church model and go after G2s and G1s—even in the absence of fathers—we can become spiritual fathers to them. We can create a sense of identity and destiny in them that changes the course of their lives. It could bring a revolution.

Paul told the Corinthian church that he believed in making a spiritual investment as a spiritual father; however, he didn't know many others doing ministry at that level.

> *For even if you were to have ten thousand teachers [to guide you] in Christ, yet you would not have many fathers [who led you to Christ and assumed responsibility for you], for I became your father in Christ Jesus through the good news [of salvation].* (1 Corinthians 4:15, AMPC)

I am so thankful for John Gimenez, who was my pastor when I got saved in 1972. He was a former heroin addict who had been in and out of prison; but he was the man I needed. I knew that if a guy like him could survive all that, he was a winner in God, and I would be a winner, too—if I submitted to John as my father. Many of today's churches are ignoring the G2 generation by segregating them from adults in a fun-focused "youth group" that's going nowhere. They receive no substance of the reality of God, and are asked to do no work in the church.

Why They Come Back After College

The G2 generation can become a force if we rescue them from youth rooms and put them to work. Pastors can inspire them with messages about the greatness of God. We can sow vision into them by telling them they have a destiny. We can give them opportunities to serve. Then, we can reverse the trend of kids going away to college and never coming back.

When the G2s have church responsibilities, they aren't passive. They don't avoid church. Just the opposite. They push their parents to come on time because they are serving this Sunday and don't want to be late. It's awesome! If you took our G2's into separate rooms, asked them about the vision and ministries at Rock City Church, and then compared their responses to the answers, you would say, "Did they get a script?" All of their answers would be basically the same. People come to me and say, "When I talk to your young people, it's like talking to you."

So many churches experience the pain of watching their best, most energized youth grow up and move out. We are confident that the 5-G Shift is one of the secrets that makes RCC so effective in the community, and so enduring as a ministry. We transfer a different spirit to the G2s than what they're receiving from the culture. They get a different spirit from the older generations of saints by transpneumigration, the laying on of hands, and the release into ministry. We do not coddle them, entertain them, or spoil them; so we do not lose them!

Once we believe in G2s, father them, and give them something important to do, they'll love being in the House of God more than anything else. *This chapter focuses specifically on them—the G2 generation.*

G2s Are Young Adults, Not Older Children

A century ago, teenagers weren't regarded as children during the final phase of childhood; they were adults in the early years of adulthood: "young adults."

Back in 1997, God shook up Rock City Church in Baltimore when He showed me what I was doing wrong by having a separate youth ministry. As a result, I began to focus on G2s as young adults, not as children. Our young adults grew quickly; each one discovered a unique call of God on their lives, and they stayed and worked in our 5-G Local Church to fulfill it.

The Bible says that David served the Lord in his generation (Acts 13:36). David was still a G2 when Samuel anointed him as future king of Israel. He was a teenager, but he was already a responsible and courageous shepherd who could be trusted to watch his father's sheep. He was capable of killing wild animals who tried to attack. When he went before King Saul and convinced him that he could fight Goliath, he already had a testimony.

God can use anyone He wants to use. Throughout history, He's often used youth—people that, today, we consider "too young." The Bible says, "God is the Judge! He puts down one and lifts up another" (Psalm 75:7, AMPC).

David, Gideon, Esther, Isaac, and the young kings of Israel were all G2s when they answered the call of God. God doesn't use the teen years for fun and games. Those are warrior years, because the G2s have fewer distractions, such as raising a family, which come later. They're available for ministry, and can be undivided in their devotion.

An unmarried man is concerned about the Lord's affairs—how he can please the Lord. But a married man is concerned about the affairs of this world— how he can please his wife—and his interests are divided. An unmarried woman or virgin is concerned about the Lord's affairs: Her aim is to be devoted to the Lord in both body and spirit. But a married woman is concerned about the affairs of this world—how she can please her husband. I am saying this for your own good, not to restrict you, but that you may live in a right way in undivided devotion to the Lord. (1 Corinthians 7:32-35, NIV)

Coming of Age Celebrations in the 5-G Local Church

At Rock City Church, when our children become 12 years old, we celebrate the transition with a special time during a Sunday service when we bring them up on stage. We have their biography, and details about what they want to do as an adult—what ministry they want to join in our church. During that service, they give me a toy that they've had since childhood.

When I was a child, I talked like a child, I thought like a child, I reasoned like a child; when I became a man, I did away with childish things. (1 Corinthians 13:11, AMPC)

In return, I give them a shopping bag full of ministry-focused items that include a new Bible, gift cards from stores that represent their new G2 Christian lifestyle, and other items. This presentation is similar to a bar mitzvah, when a Jewish child is welcomed into adulthood.

Coming of age as a G2 means that you leave things behind that represent your childhood, and press onward and upward to the high calling of God in Christ Jesus! We've seen that, once we release these young G2 church members to begin operating in faith and zeal for the Lord and His Kingdom, they enter into the service of God full of life to do His work in His house.

Over the years of practicing this New Testament attitude toward G2s, we've seen very significant changes take place that confirm to us this is God's method and His plan. Many of our ministries are now run by former G2s who grew up in the house, went away to college, and came back to RCC to step right into their places of ministry.

Our children's director has been in the church since she was two years old. She went to college, returned, and is married with four children. She is totally committed to the vision of the house. One of our pastors has been here at RCC since he was eleven. He went away to college, returned, and is married with three children. He and his wife run The Hiding Place, our home for pregnant girls. He is a great blessing in the house and ministry. Many others have followed this pattern for years, from financial directors to audio ministry members. Our G2s have become the core leaders of our church: *this is how it should be.* That is the biblical model—not placing them into a separate youth ministry.

Modern church youth programs isolate the best, most zealous warriors from the rest of the body. This causes the fire and zeal of the G2s to diminish. It negatively affects their evangelism. It trains them to be future pew warmers, not worshipping warriors. Churches do not have to experience the pain of watching their most energized young people grow up and move away. We are confident that our commitment to the G2 generation is one of the keys that makes us effective and enduring as a church. We release our youth from the world's culture to energize the church by transpneumigration. Older saints lay hands on them and honor them as unique and valuable members of the church, releasing them into ministry.

Don't let anyone look down on you because you are young, but set an example for the believers in speech, in life, in love, in faith and in purity. (1 Timothy 4:12, NIV)

This 5-G shift in thinking toward the youth has other positive effects:

- Cultural peer pressure leads teens into compromise and impurity, but positive peer pressure in the church is a driving force for integrity and purity.
- G2s become spiritual trend-setters for G1s, because they are active in the work of the Lord.
- G2s exert influence upward to the older generations. Our G2s provoke the G3s, G4s, and G5s to renew their zeal—their energy is contagious!

The traditional youth group mentality creates a negative generation gap between teens and their parents. Parents are giving their kids up to "step" parents—youth ministers only slightly older than the teenagers. Parents have already seen their roles diminish from the adverse influence of the world's music industry, advertising industry, movies, sports, and so on. Then, they face another surrender of their parenting imposed by the church!

The church should know better. Parents make the best mentors of their own kids. The church should promote the Deuteronomy 6 pattern, wherein parents are the ones responsible for preparing G1s and G2s to pursue their God-given callings.

These words, which I am commanding you today, shall be on your heart. You shall teach them diligently to your sons and shall talk of them when you sit in your house and when you walk by the way and when you lie down and when you rise up. You shall bind them as a sign on your hand and they shall be as frontals on your forehead. You shall write them on the doorposts of your house and on your gates. (Deuteronomy 6:6-9, NASB)

When teens come to our church and their parents aren't saved, we have developed a follow-up program to reach those lost parents. We want our G2s to fully experience all of God and His purposes, and we want their parents to be born again along with them.

G2 Roles in Theatrical Productions

Every year at Rock City Church, we perform several first-class theatrical productions. Every time we do this, the production teams are predominantly G2s and early G3s.

Theatrical productions are a powerful tool for sharing the Gospel of Jesus Christ. Each event requires teams of actors, writers, editors, coaches, designers, seamstresses, stage crew, hair and makeup artists, and technical support teams in audio, video, television, lighting, and special effects. Actors get to release a joyful and powerful expression of the love of God. They are able to use their talents to tell the Good News of Jesus Christ.

Our crews work together as a spiritual force to present a compelling Gospel message and bring about God's purpose through their productions. They bring the words and message of the Bible to life, addressing modern-day issues with biblical solutions and interpretations. They find tremendous joy and satisfaction in reaching those who know Jesus and want Him more, as well as those who haven't heard the Gospel and don't know Him yet in saving grace.

One annual production has had over 140,000 people attend, with more than 9,000 souls coming to Christ.

The crews for set design, lighting and video are loaded with G2s. Many of the actors are G2s. These young adults also bring their friends to church to see the plays, and the friends give their lives to Christ. One of our parents opened her home up to her daughter's best friends to come and hang out. She always concluded their time with prayer and Bible discussion. As a result, her daughter has had an impact on her classmates that has even carried over to her college years.

The Compassion Commission

Compassion Commission[9] is a youth-led initiative to help rebuild and restore our communities. Local teens and youth ages 11 to 17, located all around the region, gather in Baltimore every July to rebuild a home for a family in need. They complete acts of service throughout the community, as well. Compassion Commission has a profound impact on both the teens who serve and the residents who benefit from their acts of kindness.

This youth missions program began 17 years ago, and is hosted by Rock City Church. Each year, hundreds of youth from all over the United States come to Baltimore to be a part of this intense and exciting conference. They learn from the Word of God, and have opportunities

9. Rock City Church Compassion Commission, Baltimore, Maryland. Online at *https://rockcitychurch.com/get-compassion-cc/* and *https://compassioncommission.wixsite.com/compassioncommission.*

to apply what they learn through a series of inner-city compassion outreach projects. These youth experience powerful times of prayer, praise, worship and ministry at a series of evening services. There are several components of this program that bring value and spiritual growth, including the following.

Giving away a home! Compassion Commission partners with Adopt-A-Block every year to rebuild a home. At the end of the week, we give that home away for free to a family that has never owned a home before. This year, we gave away our 17th home!

Promotions. Beginning in December, we send out email blasts, letters to senior pastors, and follow-up calls. We reach out to the local youth in our church, and also open up the event to out-of-town churches. Thousands of kids have attended throughout the years. G2s receive intense, hands-on training, along with several fun activities.

Goals. Youth learn how to serve others, how to lead and communicate, and how to work as a team to be effective witnesses for the Kingdom of God. The goal of the week is to reach out and touch people in the city. We also have a long-term purpose: we want to impart compassion into young people, and train them to go back into their cities clothed with compassion.

Ministry locations. To accomplish these purposes, locations are selected throughout the city of

Baltimore—places such as homeless shelters, food pantries, community centers, farms, and local parks. Here, we plan clean-up projects and presentations for the local people. The Performing Arts Team leads in worship and drama. Daily skits prepare the youth for the event's yearly theme.

Housing. Accommodations are provided for out-of-town youth and RCC youth as needed. Host homes are families from RCC who've been approved by our Pastoral Care and Finance departments. In the event that insufficient host homes are available, external sources are used.

Transportation. A large number of vehicles and drivers are needed to transport the youth to and from events and host homes. Volunteer drivers must submit a valid driver's license, driving record, and vehicle insurance.

Meals. Breakfast, lunch and dinner are covered by the registration fee and are provided for the entire week. Volunteers prepare food, set up, serve, and clean up. Packed lunches are provided on days when the youth are working off-site.

Medical coverage. A nurse and nursing station are available in the event of a medical need. Parents submit allergy forms, so that our nursing team is prepared ahead of time. Parents are notified in case of emergencies, and our nursing team is connected to a local hospital and its triage unit.

The Compassion Commission Midyear Recharge

Over the years, the lives of many youth have been radically changed at Compassion Commission. They return to their homes and schools and impact their communities with the power and love of God. However, sometimes after a few months, the fire goes out, and they lose some of the excitement for God that they received in July. They need a reminder of all God did for them during that week, and all He wants to do through them again. For this reason, we bring them together again at the beginning of each new year.

Recharge is a special youth night in January when we remember all that God did the previous July at Compassion Commission, and get the youth excited about the next conference. This one-night Recharge, hosted by the Radical Disciples, is open to previous Compassion Commission members, outside churches, new churches, Radical Disciples, and RCC members. Attendees register for the upcoming event, and make plans to go back home and invite other youth to attend.

Our expectation is that Recharge participants return home with a new, clear, fresh focus on God. They continue to impact their communities for the glory of God, and get ready to come back in July, full of zeal to change our city.

As parents and pastors, we train G2s in biblical absolutes because the generation behind us is asking, "Mom, Dad—what do you believe?" They want stability.

And wisdom and knowledge shall be the stability of thy times, and strength of salvation: the fear of the LORD is his treasure. (Isaiah 33:6, KJV)

The world needs stable Christians. Stability needs to be the walk of our life. I see too many flaky Christians who come to church for a week or two and then disappear. They serve in one area, and then they're gone. They're all over the place. They're happy one day, and depressed the next. They're unstable.

When the church is unstable, it causes a ripple effect in the culture. Stability means firmness of position, resistance to disintegration—something stable is not likely to fall, because it's firm and steady. The church needs to return to the place of stability that is found only in God—through His wisdom and knowledge, the strength of His salvation, and the fear of the Lord, which is His treasure.

Lord, Shift Us Again!

Lord, bring us again to a new place! Shift us so we'll embrace this new thing! The Bible says in Mark 16:17, "These signs shall follow those that believe." We need an awakening—a restoration of the power of God in the church. We need a fresh revelation and a divine visitation.

We have traded God's power for entertainment and amusements. God is saying that it's a new day; it's time for a shift, and we need to be a part of it. We need to start it! In Acts 2:39, it says that God will pour out His Spirit on our children, our children's children, and those yet to be born. God wants to send His power into every generation.

When I was a young man in the G2 generation, I laid hands on a baby who had no irises, and the irises grew in her eyes! God changed my life at that moment, because power was in my hands. God wants to fill you with the Holy Ghost and give you power.

I believe that the new reformation God wants to bring through the church will shift the culture of America. This shift lies within the revelation and acceptance of this reproductive message of generational thinking. We can't wait for the culture to shift and shift the church with it. No, we need to shift first, and have the culture catch up to us. The church needs to revisit this subject of intentional generational impact that concluded the Old Testament and introduced the New.

Behold, I will send you Elijah the prophet before the great and terrible day of the Lord comes. He shall turn and reconcile the hearts of the [estranged] fathers to the [ungodly] children, and the hearts of the [rebellious] children to their fathers [a reconciliation produced by repentance of the ungodly], lest I come and smite the land with a curse. (Malachi 4:5-6, AMPC)

John the Baptist came in the spirit and power of Elijah to turn the hearts of the fathers to the children (Luke 1:17). Do you see this power in the church today? Why have we moved away from that revelation? The restoration of spiritual mothers and fathers in the Body of Christ will do so much to impact generations and give them true identity in Christ.

Children who run around wondering if they're a boy or a girl don't have identity. Fathers give children identity. We need to bring back the identity that comes from learning about life from your father. Even when natural fathers are missing, the church should always be relied upon to provide spiritual fathers, especially to the impressionable G2s and G1s.

A remnant of G2s will arise out of the dust heap of the culture that is currently in such disarray. These G2s will not be satisfied until they have an impact for Christ. I am excited for them, and I want to help them hit their stride and succeed. I hope and pray that you will help them also.

Throughout this book, I have issued a challenge to the older generations—G3, G4, and G5—to transfer their spirits to the G2s so that they become guardians of their streets and schools. I said that, if we impart supernatural power into our Christian youth and call them into the ministry, they will deal with the devil and bring revival. If you are reading this book and you are G3 or G4, you may be thinking, "Well, I did well with a youth pastor 30 or 40 years ago."

My response to that is, "Well, I didn't wear seat belts back then, either."

We have moved into a new day and a new time. Like the children of Issachar, we must know the season and the times, and understand what we ought to do (1 Chronicles 12:32).

A serious work is ahead for the church. We must follow the Apostle Paul's admonition:

For I am confident of this very thing, that He who began a good work in you will perfect it until the day of Christ Jesus." (Philippians 1:6, NASB)

chapter 7

The 5-G Local Church

"When Jesus heard this, He said to him, 'You still lack one thing; sell everything that you have and distribute the money to the poor, and you will have [abundant] treasure in heaven; and come, follow Me [becoming My disciple, believing and trusting in Me and walking the same path of life that I walk].' But when he heard these things, he became very sad, for he was extremely rich." (Luke 18:22-23, AMPC)

WHEN THE RICH young ruler was talking to Jesus, the Bible says the discussion stopped as soon as the subject of money came up. That's exactly what happens in churches all around the world whenever it's time for the offering. Jesus told the man to release his money and follow Him, but the man said no. He wanted to keep his money, even if he lost the chance to follow Jesus.

What went wrong? The whole time Jesus was talking to him, another voice inside the man was disagreeing with Jesus. It was the voice of mammon—the demonic spirit attached to money, that seemed louder than the voice of Jesus. Jesus was standing there in person, and the man turned him down. He couldn't give up his bondage to that other god.

Mammon always opposes the voice of the true God. Jesus said that you can serve either God or mammon. You can't do both. Either you release your money to Jesus for whatever ministry purpose he designates, and walk in freedom, or you keep your money and stay in bondage.

No man can serve two masters: for either he will hate the one, and love the other; or else he will hold to the one, and despise the other. Ye cannot serve God and mammon. (Matthew 6:24, KJV)

This chapter is about the 5-G Local Church model we've developed in Baltimore, Maryland, on the biblical basis of generational transfer from one generation to another, the love of Jesus, and the principles of His Word. We have ministries for the poor. We produce plays. We start churches and have our own Bible school. We develop youth into future leaders. We have a children's ministry, a children's academy, and a sports ministry for kids. We've walked out our pro-life commitment by establishing a home for pregnant girls. We are able to do all of this not only because our people pray and come to church and try to follow what I teach, but because our people give.

Ministry takes money. That means, at some point, you will have to confront the god of mammon in your people. Some will reject you, just as the rich young ruler rejected Jesus. Some may leave your church. But another group will arise that says, "Yes!" They will choose to obey God, not mammon. They will be your righteous core.

God is greater than the spirit of mammon, which messes with your mind and tries to prevent you from listening to Jesus' voice. When you serve mammon, it will come about that, just as you are about to do a God thing, the spirit of mammon will tell you not to do it. You'll be ready to step out in faith, but mammon will say, "No." So you won't. That is the power of the mammon spirit.

Jesus made that rich man a life-changing offer—an offer that I accepted decades ago. I have not regretted it. I know many others who have made the same choice. I said yes to Jesus when He told me to release my money to Him. Multiple translations and Bible dictionaries confirm that mammon is the god of riches. Mammon is a "Chaldee or Syriac word meaning 'wealth' or 'riches' (Luke 16:9-11); also, by personification, the god of riches (Matthew 6:24; Luke 16:9-11)."[10] Mammon is a demonic spirit.

---

10. *Easton's Bible Dictionary and Webster's Unabridged Dictionary.* Online at *https://biblehub.com/topical/m/mammon.htm.*

For the love of money is the root of all evil: which while some coveted after, they have erred from the faith, and pierced themselves through with many sorrows. (1 Timothy 6:10, KJV)

You need to help your people conquer the spirit of mammon by teaching them to give freely before God has to deal with them Himself. This is how you will be prepared to flourish as a 5-G Local Church.

Do not be deceived and deluded and misled; God will not allow Himself to be sneered at (scorned, disdained, or mocked by mere pretensions or professions, or by His precepts being set aside.) [He inevitably deludes himself who attempts to delude God.] For whatever a man sows, that and that only is what he will reap. (Galatians 6:7, AMPC)

Reaching the Cities Through Sports

One day, I went looking for a new baseball field. I'd founded Christian Youth Athletics (CYA)[11] in 1978 to provide youth with an opportunity to play competitive sports in a positive, Christ-centered environment. That day, I had hundreds of kids who wanted to play ball; but it was Friday, and we had been bumped from our field again. On Saturday morning, they would have no place to play. I was tired of that.

---

11. Christian Youth Athletics, Baltimore, Maryland. Online at *https://cyabaltimore.com/*.

On a hunch, I went to Armistead Gardens, an old rotten place with a lumpy field where we used to play. When I walked out onto the field, I saw a big old guy with a deep voice playing ball with some kids. He was knocking the ball out to them, and they were catching it and throwing it back. As soon as the ball came near me, I grabbed it, and I wouldn't give it back. He said, "Hey, man, give me the ball!"

I said, "No, buddy. We're going to talk first."

He marched over like he was a tough guy, but I said, "Listen. Why don't you take your kids and join up with my teams, and we'll build a new ballpark here? I'll help you build it." His name was Gil. It turned out that he was a funny guy who headed up the local Baltimore Colts Fan Club, and did a lot of other things that I found out about later. He was interested; sure enough, we teamed up.

Because of my background in construction, I was able to pull together some contractors who came in and put down new dirt and set up backstops for the new field. Gil was so blown away that he came to church just to check me out. When he came, he got saved and joined the church. The healthiest church for new believers is a 5-G Local Church, because of the nurturing environment. Gil stayed with us for the rest of his life. I married him and his wife, and helped him start a business—a tremendous business, actually.

Christian Youth Athletics provides an environment where youth learn about life in addition to sports. They develop positive relationships as they play baseball, basketball, softball, and soccer. It also gives us an opportunity to meet people like Gil. CYA coaches receive criminal background screening. They consistently demonstrate that they're men and women of integrity, walking according to biblical principles, with exemplary morals active in their lives. Because of their Christian leadership, they protect kids and show them a lifestyle free from bullying, negativity, and fighting.

CYA establishes relationships with other local churches, community organizations, and recreation leagues. Business sponsors support our teams by assisting with league expenses, equipment, and scholarships for children in need of financial assistance. We recognize their contributions through our website, league banners, season program, and team uniform shirts.

For many years, CYA has partnered with the Baltimore Orioles and Baltimore Blast to provide more exciting opportunities for the kids. G1 and G2 kids not only engage in competitive athletics, but also interact with professional athletes who encourage them to live positive, productive lives and strive for excellence—on and off the field.

Compassion costs something. It costs the church to establish ministries of compassion. However, the 5-G

Local Church believes that compassion is our Christ-like calling, and we are willing to pay for it financially. Too many people go to church only for themselves. They don't want to release their money to pay for something that benefits others. However, in a 5-G Local Church, where people have conquered the spirit of mammon, it is our greatest pleasure to give and change others' lives in the Lord's spirit of compassion.

The LORD's lovingkindnesses indeed never cease, For His compassions never fail. (Lamentations 3:22, NASB)

Christian Urban Renewal

God said that rebuilding cities is the work of believers—not politicians. We are the Lord's people, who remember Him in everything we do. The 5-G Local Church restores and rebuilds old, ruined cities, and restores the desolation of generations in the name of the Lord.

And they shall rebuild the ancient ruins; they shall raise up the former desolations and renew the ruined cities, the devastations of many generations. (Isaiah 61:4, AMPC)

God gives His people the power to create wealth, so Christians ought to be wealth builders.

But thou shalt remember the LORD thy God: for it is he that giveth thee power to get wealth, that he may establish his covenant which he swore unto thy fathers. (Deuteronomy 8:18, KJV)

When Christians get wealth and give it to the church, the church looks at the ruined cities and has the money to transform them. The church looks at the desolate generations and is able to revive them. It's able to say to those places, "We are the solution. You need to come to us."

Money for Ministry from Business Owners in the Church

My pastor, John Gimenez, was way ahead of his time. One thing he taught me, when I was a young Christian in Virginia Beach, was the importance of owning a business. He sent me to Waco, Texas, where I was trained on how to sell and present church furniture. I learned how to sell pews, pulpits, baptismal tanks, and other things churches needed. Then, he sent me to Tennessee to learn to sell office furniture, dining tables and chairs, and other items.

I started a company called New Jerusalem Church Furniture. I'd go to churches moving into a new building and give them significant discounts. The Lord used that to bless the churches, and to bless me, in all kinds of ways, including developing a personal family income. I was able to lead the church without the conflict of being dependent on church offerings for personal survival.

Brother John asked me to teach 100 other pastors how to start businesses, too. Today, I expect all of the pastors under me to start businesses. We teach a curriculum called Steps to Victory, which covers church financial issues that pastors deal with every day—skills such as administration, investment, and bookkeeping. This program also teaches them how to start and run a business themselves, as well as how to help their members start them. When pastors and members prosper financially, the whole church prospers and can build and sustain ministries that renew cities for God.

God owns all the money on earth; we are only stewards submitted to Him. It's not our money; we are simply managing it for Him. Money cannot buy salvation, grace, healing, deliverance, or any other blessing from God. However, God can learn a lot about you from how you handle money. Mammon tries to keep money on top, but God says money is on the bottom: it's the least important thing in your life. Jesus said this:

He that is faithful in that which is least is faithful also in much: and he that is unjust in the least is unjust also in much. (Luke 16:10, KJV)

The Glorious Church

I was standing at the front of the church on my wedding day. There, at the back of the church, I was thrilled to see my bride, Coralee, walk in. She was standing with her dad, dressed in a beautiful white wedding gown, ready to walk down the aisle to become my wife.

I want to ask you something. If Coralee had fallen in the mud a few minutes earlier and wrinkled her gown and spotted it with dirt, do you think I would have called off the wedding? Certainly not! I might have needed to help her clean up a bit, but that wedding would still have taken place. She was my bride, and on that day, she would become my wife.

The Bible says that the Church is the Bride and Jesus is the Bridegroom, preparing us for the wedding.

And I saw the holy city, the new Jerusalem, descending out of heaven from God, all arrayed like a bride beautified and adorned for her husband. (Revelation 21:2, AMPC)

Since the Church was formed, it has become soiled and wrinkled; but Jesus is not changing His mind. He is committed to cleaning us up and marrying us. We will be a glorious church because of Him—He will make us perfect in every way.

Husbands, love your wives, even as Christ also loved the church, and gave himself for it; that he might sanctify and cleanse it with the washing of water by the word, that he might present it to himself a glorious church, not having spot, or wrinkle, or any such thing; but that it should be holy and without blemish. (Ephesians 5:25-27, KJV)

When we see ourselves as the Bride of Christ, nothing seems impossible. Our identity comes through His example of humility, servanthood, and generational transfer to disciples. Jesus is cleaning up the spots and wrinkles; meanwhile, we have such great authority and power in the world as His glorious Church!

The Greek word I have used in this book for the 5-G generational transfer of spirit in the church is *transpneumigration*. It changes our focus from us to others because we disciple the younger generations.

Trans—move (from one place to another)

Pneuma—spirit

Migration—establish a new residence in the place where you have moved.

Churches Build Leaders by Discipleship

When I started pastoring Rock City Church[12] in the 1980s, we didn't have multiple generations available for transfer because we didn't have many people other than G2s. I took a group of about 40 G2s into my house every Friday night for three years and poured into them what a life with God could be. My home was not the sterile environment of a strict classroom setting;

---

12. Rock City Church, Baltimore, Maryland. Online at *https://rockcitychurch.com/*.

it was a natural setting. Some were laying on the floor. Some were sitting on pillows. They were sitting all over my house, and we were eating popcorn and having dessert while I taught the Word.

As we multiplied and grew, the group expanded and became actively involved in the church and the community ministries we started. Many of those original G2s are my elders today. They're the leaders in my church. Their commitment causes our church and ministries to succeed. A 5-G Local Church sets up opportunities for each member to use their gifts and be trained. The evidence of perfection in your walk with God is revealed as you learn and practice what you have learned.

God doesn't expect local churches to be stuck in a Sunday service mentality, where the pastor repeats and repeats and repeats the same things every week. In a 5-G Local Church, pastors are spiritual fathers and mothers focused on discipleship and the releasing of people into new ministry opportunities. They know the vision of the house, and they live out what they've learned.

In recent years, too many pastors have become like nannies and instructors with no strong spiritual investment in their members and attendees. They don't move past outward traditions. As a result, the Gospel is made of no effect. That's why we need a 5-G Shift. We need to teach the generations behind us what it means to be a real Christian. We need to impart a new spirit through transpneumigration.

Church Succession by Spiritual Fathering

When you're a 5-G Local Church pastor, you are a parent taking responsibility for the Christian growth of younger generations. You teach them what God has done in the past and encourage them to become active in the things of God now. Biblical examples of spiritual fathers and sons are Elijah and Elisha, Paul and Timothy, and Moses and Joshua.

The Bible says Joshua failed to pass on to the next generation what God had done. As a result, a decline began in Israel: kings came into leadership instead of prophets. Joshua had received it from Moses, but he didn't pass it on.

The people served the LORD all the days of Joshua, and all the days of the elders who survived Joshua, who had seen all the great work of the LORD which He had done for Israel. Then Joshua the son of Nun, the servant of the LORD, died at the age of one hundred and ten. And they buried him in the territory of his inheritance in Timnath-heres, in the hill country of Ephraim, north of Mount Gaash. All that generation also were gathered to their fathers; and there arose another generation after them who did not know the LORD, nor yet the work which He had done for Israel. (Judges 2:7-10, NASB)

In the world, succession usually means the next guy in line comes along and takes over. That might work in corporate America, when you're dealing with a product, but it doesn't work in the church. In a church, a new leader is taking on responsibility for the spiritual lives of people who are submitted to God and the pastor.

If some new prospective pastor for Rock City Church came to replace me, I could tell him about my girls' home and the feeding program where we feed thousands of people; or our block parties and giveaway of homes. However, if he had not received my spirit, he might know what I've done, but he wouldn't know how or why I did it.

Sometimes, the church thinks it can simply bring in Pastor Billy and say to Pastor Fred, "Here's your successor." Then Fred walks away, and Billy's got the church. The problem with this is that Billy has no idea how Fred did it. How many pastors do we know who've passed on churches to somebody else, and then the church fell apart? This has happened even when the new pastor is their own son or daughter. The history of that is horrible.

When you are a 5-G, discipleship-based local pastor who's imparted your spirit to the younger generations, you have lots of people who could replace you, because you went vertical instead of horizontal. The vertical vision of the house went down from top to bottom—from you to those coming after you. Whoever comes along can follow what you started, because everybody knows and practices the vision, which you've faithfully been building on a biblical foundation of discipleship.

What We Learned from Russia After the Iron Curtain

In 1989, when the former Soviet Union broke up and the Iron Curtain came down, I went with Bob Weiner, David Kiteley, and other Christian leaders to Moscow to preach the Gospel. We returned again and again over a period of several years; eventually, we were able to lead over 10,000 students to Christ. We soon became aware that these students needed to be discipled and trained to be the new church leaders of the former Soviet Union. We wanted the curriculum to fit into their culture and their current needs.

We saw the impact of the schools. We were training those who were really called, not those who were simply looking to go to a Bible school to get knowledge. Our students wanted to be practitioners, not theorists. We saw tremendous development.

We started with 35 students in our first class. From that group, we began to plant churches. We planted about 125 churches all over the former Soviet Union and the Ukraine. We brought this model back to the United States and started a school in Virginia Beach, Virginia. Then, we brought it to Baltimore. We trained small groups of American and international students from Madagascar, Ghana, Malawi, Cameroon,

Ukraine, India, Indonesia and Switzerland. One school in Madagascar has graduated about 250 students and planted 15 churches.

We recorded videos of our Bible school teachers, and took them to other nations to start Bible schools there. They dubbed the videos locally into their native languages. The benefits of empowering internationals continue to reap results.

Training for Christian Ministry in the 5-G Local Church

Rock City Church is located in Cromwell Valley, in the northern part of Baltimore, also known as Towson. This area is rich in Christian heritage. Followers of John Wesley and George Whitefield preached here. Robert Strawbridge held camp meetings, and Billy Sunday won multitudes to Christ. Many have gone before us, and many more will follow. As a 5-G Local Church, we are continuing that Christian legacy by training teachers for the future generations. We are transferring to them what we have become in Christ.

A pupil is not above his teacher; but everyone, after he has been fully trained, will be like his teacher. (Luke 6:40, NASB)

Our desire is to set a mark on many lives so that they can go to many places, fulfilling God's great commission to reach those who still need to hear. We instruct, train, and equip men and women to be effective ministers. Whether they are in the marketplace or full time ministry, they will be righteous and wise in the wisdom of God.

Give instruction to a wise man and he will be still wiser, teach a righteous man and he will increase his learning. (Proverbs 9:9, NASB)

We all know that it takes more than one Sunday service a week to empower people to find God's purpose for their lives and become equipped to fulfill that purpose. We started Cromwell Christian School of Ministry (CCSM)[13] to equip students to find and fulfill their calling in God and to reap the coming harvest. Our goal is to develop Christian students into soldiers—strong citizens of the Kingdom of God—who not only know the Word, but also put it into immediate use in their work and their behavior.

Teach them his decrees and instructions, and show them the way they are to live and how they are to behave. (Exodus 18:20, NIV)

We decided from the beginning that CCSM would be a citywide Bible training center, serving the entire Metropolitan Baltimore area. We believe it requires a citywide church to reap a citywide harvest, which, ultimately, can spread to the world. The citywide church is a

---

13. Cromwell Christian School of Ministry, Baltimore, Maryland. Online at *https://rockcitychurch.com/grow-in-god/*.

formidable force of talent, diversity, gifting, and anointing. The church is unified, so its strength is multiplied as it raises up leaders.

Each year, we hold an Intensive Training School (ITS)—a balance between the spiritual and practical components of ministry. Ministry Preparation consists of two tracks: Full-time Vocational Ministry and Marketplace Ministry. Everyone benefits from an infusion of fresh insight and revelation.

At CCSM, we've experienced a realm in God that we previously did not know was obtainable. We have come into a place of His overwhelming and consuming presence. We've learned about worshipping at His feet, as Mary did, and also serving, as Martha did. We incorporate these two practices into our routines in this way:

Mary—at His feet in the morning. In the first part of the day, we follow the Mary phase, sitting at His feet to learn of Him.

Martha—practicing what you have learned in the afternoon. Later in the day, students walk out what they have learned in a practicum of Christian service, or the Martha phase. This is designed to develop a ministry of compassion through hands-on serving. Students are exposed to a wide range of activities that empower them in effective city-taking strategies.

Jesus loved to go to the home of Mary, Martha, and Lazarus. As much as He loved the worship and adoration,

He also loved the welcome and warm reception of Martha's meals. She knew how to entertain her Savior and how to host His majesty. When we learn to worship like Mary and serve like Martha, we just might get Lazarus to come forth. Lazarus was dead—as is much of the world's population. This world is desperately waiting to hear of a living and loving God who dwells in the midst of His people. We must take the burning passion in our hearts to those in our lost and dying world. This is the heartbeat of Cromwell Christian School of Ministry.

Children's Academic Education in a 5-G Local Church

Churches that rose up after the slavery era became the centers of each black community. These churches continued to provide spiritual strength, as the underground church had done during slavery. They also took practical steps on behalf of their people. Public education in the South was rare in those days, even for poor white children. Blacks, of course, were treated even worse. That was where the black churches stepped in to restore the desolation of former generations. You can imagine how little money they had, having just been released from bondage; but they weren't controlled by the spirit of mammon. They gave all that they had.

Some assistance came from the American Missionary Association, the Federal Freedman's Bureau, and other benefactors. Still, those black churches led the way, raising money to start local schools for their children. They defeated illiteracy within the first generation after slavery! Nothing like it has ever happened before or since. If that vision was restored today, inner cities could change overnight through Christian academic education paid for by the church.

At Rock City Church, the academic education of our children is of vital importance. We spare no expense or effort in training and developing our little ones. We take responsibility for their academic education, like those churches of the past. We train them up in the way they should go, that when they get old they will not depart from the truth (see Proverbs 22:6). Our admissions process is designed to ensure each student a successful and rewarding experience.

Since 1983, Rock Christian Academy[14] has educated hundreds of children. We have an exceptional school, with a proven history of high standards and academic excellence. Our students test higher than students in other comparable academic programs. Many of our alumni today serve in positions of leadership throughout the community as principals, teachers, military officers, business owners, musicians, and more. Jesus said,

---

14. Rock City Church Academy, Baltimore, Maryland. Online at *https://rockchurchacademy.com/*.

Suffer the little children to come unto me, and forbid them not: for of such is the kingdom of God. (Mark 10:14, KJV)

We welcome children, and train them to be originals who understand their God-given purposes. We refuse to allow the secular culture to shape them into its image. Because we are a 5-G Local Church, we develop younger generations into leaders for tomorrow—anchored in Christ, geared to impact the culture, and walking confidently in their God-given purposes. Our approach to learning focuses on developing the whole child: academically, socially, emotionally, physically, and spiritually. We believe the school is an extension of both home and church in its objective to train up children "in the way they should go."

Our well-rounded instructional approach fosters critical thinking, communication, character development, learning through play, and focuses on STEAM subjects (Science, Technology, Engineering, Arts, Math) in a safe, nurturing learning environment. We provide small group instruction and individualization. We also offer opportunities for working parents to register for extended day care before and after school.

Rock City Church Academy is registered with the Maryland State Department of Education. We are active members of the Association of Christian Schools

International (ACSI). Our private campus is monitored by video screening and routine perimeter surveillance. Entrances are locked during school hours to prevent access to students. All staff are CPR/First Aid Certified, and trained on how to best respond to emergencies in accordance with our School Emergency Action Plan. All of our staff have undergone a rigorous background screening and character evaluation process to ensure that they are qualified to work with children in the character of Christ.

Radical Youth Ministry in a 5-G Local Church

As you will recall, I shared that Rock City Church, years ago, abandoned the model of youth ministry that required a youth pastor—a model that separates teenagers from their parents and the rest of the church. At RCC, we're committed to developing the youth in our church to become all they are called to be. We don't babysit youth or become substitute parents. Instead, we empower parents to train up their children in the way that they should go, so that when they are old they will not depart from it. We do this in several concrete ways:

Training for ministry. The youth at RCC don't need to sit and wait for their turn to minister. They complete a course in First Principles (foundational doctrines of the Bible) and are encouraged to serve in ministry. We teach them about lifelong disciplines that cultivate their personal relationship with Jesus. These include a daily prayer life and daily time in the Word, as well as faithful attendance at church services.

Radical Disciples (youth leaders). Radical Disciples are core youth leaders, trained to be harvesters in the Kingdom of God. They labor and produce fruit for future generations. These harvesters are the future of the church and all that God wants to do on the earth. They are not just inheritors, sitting back and consuming what God has done in the past. Rather, they are paving the way for what God will do in generations to come.

Planning meetings. Radical Disciples are responsible for planning events for youth nights and other youth functions throughout the year. Meetings are held once a month to find creative ways to engage the youth and help them to plug into the church.

Activities and monthly youth nights. Radical Disciples activities are times when youth have fun and fellowship as they build relationships with one another. These times also include opportunities to become better equipped in the Word of God. Radicals/Youth Nights are scheduled the last Friday of the month. During the month of November, Radical Disciples also serve at the Adopt-A-Block Thanksgiving dinner.

Adopting Local Neighborhoods

One of the citywide coalition partnerships we've developed as a 5-G Local Church is called Adopt-A-Block[15], a 501(c)(3) charitable organization. We work with other local churches, city governments, the police department, local businesses, community associations, social service and health agencies, and area residents to bring restoration to our city—block by block.

Each year, we host five to eight block parties in some of the highest crime areas of Baltimore's Eastern District. Our goal is to effectively meet the spiritual, emotional, mental, and physical needs of families, parents, children, seniors, and individuals. Here are some examples:

- Adopt-A-Block
- Block Party in East Baltimore
- A Can Can Make A Difference (food collection and giveaways)
- Christian Youth Athletics
- Compassion Commission (see Chapter 6)

Each event requires many people, and a lot of planning, to come to life. Here are the practical steps we take to make these events happen:

1. Unity, Preparation, and Logistics

Adopt-A-Block events unify various representatives from agencies, churches, and community associations.

---

15. Adopt-A-Block, Baltimore, Maryland. Online at *www.adoptablock-inc.com/*.

We identify local pastors in the neighborhood who are able to provide ongoing spiritual guidance. We share with them details they may not know about regarding how to identify community needs and link residents to services in the areas of health, jobs, and substance abuse treatment.

Working together, we make preparations and determine logistics for the Adopt-A-Block event:

- Plan the day's program—who will perform, speak, sing, dance, act, and so on
- Promote the Block Party with banners, balloons, flyers, and media coverage
- Contact dignitaries, from the police district commander and the fire chief to elected officials citywide
- Send teams of prayer warriors onto the block and surrounding areas to pray and pass out literature promoting the event
- Plan booths to address immediate and long-term needs
- Local churches and community associations
- Health care—blood pressure and eye screening, addiction treatment organizations, local clinics, and health care providers
- Education—GED, college recruiters, literacy and reading programs
- Identify block leaders who can manage a follow-up program for change and renewal in the area (In

some cases, we obtain a house and move someone in to fulfill this role.)

2. Invasion

On the day of the Adopt-A-Block Event, we create a party atmosphere with performers and fun activities. We set up booths on the streets to hand out groceries, clothing, hot dogs, and drinks. Other booths link people to local churches and organizations providing addiction treatment, child services, community contacts, employment, education, and medical care.

3. Occupation (follow-up)

After the Adopt-A-Block event, we follow up and establish a permanent presence on that block to continue the work the Lord has begun. Adoption is incomplete unless there is a successful occupation of the block. No matter how successful the Block Party has been, it is ultimately the follow-up program that reveals the true impact.

There are four main ingredients to an effective adoption—people, commitment, unity, and relationships. Mixing all four together in the right blend helps to create vision, and provide services needed by area residents and their surrounding neighborhoods.

Some follow-up services that we may coordinate include these:

- Transportation to church

- Personal visits to families on the block
- Immediate needs like home repair, food, clothes, shelter, substance abuse treatment, crisis intervention, and job assistance
- Prayer and Bible study
- GED and educational programs
- Contact for community agencies
- Counseling
- Youth programs
- Outdoor Sunday School

Pro-Life Solutions in a 5-G Local Church

Many Christians feel strongly about ending abortion, but few local churches recognize that the church is the best-equipped organization to reverse the trend and restore respect and reverence for life. Lasting solutions to ending abortion are not political or judicial but biblical. The 5-G Local Church is the solution. Everything will change when the 5-G Local Church gets vitally involved, because God is with us. He is the Creator of life.

Before I formed you in the womb I knew you, and before you were born I consecrated you; I have appointed you a prophet to the nations. (Jeremiah 1:5, NASB)

The church is the best place for a successful pro-life ministry, because churches can boldly promote biblical principles, from forgiveness in Christ and mercy to sinners to the future of the family on the earth. The Church can speak publicly from a Christian perspective when issues are raised about so-called "rights" that conflict with the Bible and creative order.

For You formed my inward parts; You wove me in my mother's womb. I will give thanks to You, for I am fearfully and wonderfully made. (Psalm 139:13-14, NASB)

In 1985, we opened a facility called The Hiding Place[16], a nonprofit 501(c)(3) residential facility where we assist young women facing crisis pregnancy, domestic violence, substance abuse, or homelessness. The Hiding Place provides women with access to community resources, educational support, job-skills training, employment resources, and parenting support.

You are my hiding place; you will protect me from trouble and surround me with songs of deliverance. (Psalm 32:7, NASB)

At The Hiding Place, we love the women, care for them, and encourage them in a healthy Christian family environment. Thousands of young women have found our home to be a true hiding place from the crises and

16. The Hiding Place, Towson, Maryland. Online at *http://hiding-placemd.com/*.

challenges of life. More than 1,200 babies have been born! Because of our biblical commitment to families, we've encouraged and assisted these mothers to keep their babies after they are born. Most of them have done just that. It's amazing to see how the lives of everyone involved have been transformed by the love of Christ.

Young, expectant women, regardless of race or religion, who possess the desire to be helped and who agree to abide by the rules of the house, can receive help. The women begin The Hiding Place program as "Buds" and transition through a series of impartation and training opportunities to graduate as "Roses." Each woman is assigned a support family or individual who befriends, encourages, and assists her during her stay at The Hiding Place. The Hiding Place is a home structure with daily work/recreational routines. During this time, women also receive support in the form of counseling and specialized medical and educational care to prepare them for the births of their babies. This is followed by a time of transition to their own living spaces after completion of the program.

We also encourage women to continue their education. Tutoring and academic counseling are provided. In addition to helping each young lady further her education, The Hiding Place connects with local businesses, agencies, and partners who provide a variety of enrichment opportunities for young ladies. These opportunities enable them to further their skills through career counseling, job training, computer literacy, business start-ups, finances, life-skills, healthy living, fitness, parenting, and child development.

Homeless Shelter Sponsored by a 5-G Local Church

In 1991, we opened the Nehemiah House to aid adult homeless men by identifying and addressing problems that caused them to become homeless. Although the home is not currently operating, we were able to assist many men to confront addictions and find employment. We partnered with the local Veteran's Hospitals for emergency shelter needs, as well as other VA resources.

Get Ready for Revival—Take Up Your Cross

In a 5-G Local Church, Christianity never seems boring or empty. It stays fresh and hot, because you're not just going through the motions. You are following the dynamic pattern the Lord gave us when He created the Church.

In the Old Testament, the priests had to keep the fire going in the temple 24 hours a day, seven days a week. We also need to keep our fire going 24/7. That takes effort. Jesus said, "Take up your cross." That's your cross, not His. His cross was something He had to do for us. Our cross is something we do for others.

That's what makes Christianity exciting. That's how we keep the fire burning.

First, we live for Christ. We love God with all of our heart, soul, strength, and mind. Then we love our neighbors as ourselves. That's the pattern of a 5-G Local Church. We equip and train the next generation of leaders and workers for the coming harvest. We expect revival to sweep this country and nations of the world. We believe that we are on the edge of a coming move of God unlike anything we have seen before.

We must be ready for revival. That is why we need to perfect the church and equip the body of Christ for the Great Commission of Matthew 28 given to us by Jesus—a charge to teach and preach the Word and make disciples of all men. The church needs a reigniting of hearts; we need to remember that there is no higher calling—nothing more challenging to do with your life, and nothing else more long-lasting and life-changing—than serving the Lord in full-time ministry in the church.

The work before us is great. The harvest is ready. Together, we can make a difference in the Kingdom of God.